Davenport's Massachusetts Wills And Estate Planning Legal Forms

DAVENPORT'S MASSACHUSETTS WILLS AND ESTATE PLANNING LEGAL FORMS

2024 EDITION

written by attorneys Alex Russell and Robert Maxwell

SEE BOOKS AND LEGAL FORMS AT WWW.DAVENPORTPUBLISHING.COM

COPYRIGHT © 2024 -- ALEX RUSSELL

CREATIVE COMMONS LICENSE. This work is also licensed under a Creative Commons Attribution-NonCommercial-NoDerivatives 4.0 International License.

GOVERNMENT WORKS. No claim is made to copyright or ownership of government materials.

SOME STANDARD FORMS. No copyright or ownership is claimed of "standard" forms or leading forms for the state which are provided in this book, but fair use and privilege to use is claimed. Makers of such forms (often a state agency or hospital) have agreed by word, act, and implication the forms may be used and copied if no profit is sought and no substantial changes made to them. Such makers if not a lawyer or law firm are barred from profit or advantage in practicing law by making forms then limiting use. Forms and other related materials are used here for educational purposes only. Authors strongly believe in a religious duty to help people and do charity.

PUBLICATION DATA
(informal, library may use different data)

Names: Russell, Alex, 1972- author; Maxwell, Robert, 1960- author

Title: Davenport's Massachusetts Wills And Estate Planning Legal Forms 2024 Edition

Other Titles: Davenport's Wills

Description: Davenport Publishing 2024

Suggested Identifiers: 9798370550485,
LCCN 2021909030,
9798748423373

Subjects: LCSH: Wills--United States;
Wills--United States--Forms;
Estate Planning--United States;
Legal Forms

Classification: LFF KF755 .C55 2024 (or as library chooses)
DDC 346.73 Rus--dc24 (or as library chooses)

9 8 7 6 5 4 3 2 1 0 0 0 0 0 2 4

PERMISSION TO COPY AND USE BOOKS FOR FREE

To help people and groups the publisher and authors of the book allow mostly free use by giving all a "Creative Commons Attribution-NonCommercial-NoDerivatives 4.0 International License". Most users face no limit on copying, using, holding in library to loan out, or giving out copies.

Basically, as the image below shows, any copying or use is OK if it still shows it is by the authors, is non-commercial (nc) with no price charged, and has no derivatives (nd) so no big changes.

(This work licensed under a Creative Commons Attribution-NonCommercial-NoDerivatives 4.0 International License.)

TO GET COPIES OF BOOKS USE WWW.DAVENPORTPUBLISHING.COM OR AMAZON.COM.

EMAIL ANY QUESTIONS TO DAVENPORTPRESS@GMAIL.COM.

WARNING

THIS PUBLICATION IS NOT A SUBSTITUTE FOR LEGAL ADVICE. Publisher and authors say and warn this publication is not giving any legal, accounting, or other professional services or advice, which if wanted can be obtained by consulting in person an attorney or some other professional. **No attorney-client relationship or any relationship creating a duty or obligation is agreed to or created by the purchase or use of this publication or forms.**

**BOOKS AND FORMS FOR OTHER STATES ARE AVAILABLE.
SEE WWW.DAVENPORTPUBLISHING.COM FOR INFORMATION.**

CHAPTER	TABLE OF CONTENTS	PAGE NUMBER
CHAPTER 1 – LIST OF FORMS, BOOK BASICS, AND INFORMATION FORM		1
CHAPTER 2 – LEGAL TERMS AND BASIC PROPERTY LAW		6
CHAPTER 3 – WILL BASICS		8
CHAPTER 4 – WILL GIFTS INCLUDING RESIDUE CLAUSE		10
CHAPTER 5 – DEBT, HOMESTEAD, MARRIAGE, AND CHILD ISSUES		15
CHAPTER 6 – BASIC IDEAS ABOUT HEALTH CARE FORMS		18

WILL RELATED FORMS

CHAPTER 7 – FORM 1: WILL (STANDARD)		19
CHAPTER 8 – FORM 2: WILL (GUARDIAN)		23
CHAPTER 9 – FORM 3: SELF-PROVING AFFIDAVIT		27
CHAPTER 10 – FORM 4: TANGIBLE PERSONAL PROPERTY MEMORANDUM		29

HEALTH CARE FORMS

CHAPTER 11 – FORM 5: HEALTH CARE PROXY		31
CHAPTER 12 – FORM 6: DO NOT RESUSCITATE		34

GIVING POWER FORMS

CHAPTER 13 – FORM 7: DURABLE POWER OF ATTORNEY		40
CHAPTER 14 – FORM 8: TEMPORARY AGENT APPOINTMENT (FOR MINOR CHILD)		42
CHAPTER 15 – FORM 9: FINAL WISHES ABOUT BODILY REMAINS		45

APPENDIX – SAMPLE FILLED OUT LEGAL FORMS		47

CHAPTER 1
LIST OF FORMS, BOOK BASICS, AND INFORMATION FORM

ESTATE PLANNING CONTROLS THINGS IF LATER ABSENT, SICK, OR DEAD

From Davenport Publishing this book covers "Estate Planning", which is a person doing legal documents to control their health care, property, money, children, and funeral if the person is later absent, sick, or dead.

ESTATE PLANNING MOSTLY IS DOING SIMPLE THINGS IN 3 AREAS

Estate Planning is mostly doing simple things in 3 areas: Will Related, Health Care, and Giving Power. This book has many legal forms specially made for Massachusetts. Most people use just a few of the forms.

WILL RELATED FORMS

Form 1. Will (Standard) – a Will (also called a "Last Will And Testament") lets a person control things after their death like who gets money and property, who is Executor, and if easier legal options can be used.

Form 2. Will (Guardian) – this is a Will with a part added to name a person to be Guardian to care for a minor child under 18 if needed (like if both parents later die) and also manage a child's property and money.

Form 3. Self-Proving Affidavit – optional form done with a Will to later help use a Will after a death.

Form 4. Tangible Personal Property Memorandum – lets a person easily add more gifts to a Will of gifts to happen after death (but it can only cover "tangible personal property" like furniture, cars, and jewelry).

HEALTH CARE FORMS

Form 5. Health Care Proxy – lets a person name someone to control health care if needed (like due to the person's later incapacity from inability to stay conscious, talk or write health care requests, or be rational) and also write some health care instructions.

Form 6. Do Not Resuscitate – these are actually 2 forms that do the serious act of immediately refusing further care, and these are short so paramedics can read them fast and they can be used outside any facility.

GIVING POWER FORMS

Form 7. Durable Power Of Attorney – lets power over money, property, and other things be shared during a person's life with a trusted person like a spouse, adult child, or friend so they can do things.

Form 8. Temporary Agent Appointment (For Minor Child) – lets a parent share power over a child under 18 with someone so they have power to make decisions about health care and other things if needed.

Form 9. Final Wishes About Bodily Remains – lets a person give instructions to later after their death control their funeral, cremation, burial, ceremonies, and other related matters.

MASSACHUSETTS LAW ON ESTATE PLANNING COVERS MOST PEOPLE HERE

This book is only for Massachusetts since Estate Planning laws and legal documents vary among states. Massachusetts law mostly applies to Estate Planning if a person: a) has their main residence here (their "domicile"), or b) resided here and left but always keeps firm plans to leave any new place (even if a person rents a home elsewhere like some students, military, and workers). Note, many people also do health care forms for the state a health facility they use is in. Most immigrants of any kind can do Estate Planning here.

PERSON HAS POWER TO CONTROL THESE THINGS BUT IT'S OFTEN NOT VITAL

Estate Planning to control health care, property, money, children, funeral, and similar things if a person is absent, sick, or dead is usually easy to do because a person legally has full power to control these things. Given this usually judges, doctors, and other people mostly just ask: "Based on what a person wrote what did they likely want done?" It is also easy to do because simple legal documents can do the things and simple words can also be used (like listing some property and putting a few names). But despite what many people say often Estate Planning is not worth a lot of effort or money since it often doesn't greatly change costs, taxes, delays, and later work that is needed. Benefits seem especially low for young people since only 4% of people die by age 50, and only 0.2% of children before age 18 have 2 parents die to need big legal help. Many people spend more energy and money on getting good life insurance to help family and friends.

BOOK IS SHORT, QUICKLY SHOWS LEGAL FORMS, AND USES EMPHASIS

This short book may read rough but it can be read fast and it also quickly shows people many legal forms. For emphasis some paragraph titles, boxes, and underlining are used, some small words are skipped, and end quote marks are put before punctuation. Though optional legal words like Will and Testator are capitalized.

THIS BOOK COVERS THE MAIN LEGAL IDEAS AND SHOULD SUIT MOST PEOPLE

This book covers the main U.S. legal ideas on Estate Planning and big ways Massachusetts law is different. This book can't cover all legal issues but should suit most people without some strange situations or wishes. Strange situations or wishes that may need research or a lawyer include: a) strange gift wishes for property and money, b) wealth over $5 million, c) big medical concerns like extreme age, d) property or money going to a person with a disability or special needs, and e) wish to move or hide assets to qualify for government help.

DOCUMENTS MAY NEED TO BE WITNESSED, NOTARIZED, AND USED RIGHT

Some legal documents to be valid need to be "witnessed", which is someone watching the person doing the form sign and then the witness signs it too. Some documents need to be "notarized" where a person who is a "notary" sees it signed and uses an ink stamp and signs too. A person who is a notary (also called a "notary public") are at some banks, brokers, insurance agents, courts, law firms, mail-copy centers, and libraries. Many people use a phonebook to find a notary willing to help. The words "subscribe" and "execute" means a person signed a document, and "acknowledgment" means a person said a signature was theirs. If a person signs a document in a foreign language it is usually still binding. In a form the word "respectively" means "in the order just stated". When filling out a form except for signatures the other parts can be filled in by anyone, and using pencil is usually fine. Later, people often try to keep the original pages and only hand out copies. Some people have everyone sign multiple copies to have many copies with ink signatures.

LEGAL FORMS CAN HELP MANY AND THIS BOOK HAS STANDARD FORMS

Legal forms are good at most things involved in Estate Planning and can make binding legal documents. Instead of legal forms a lawyer can be used for Estate Planning but this can be costly, take months of work, and they can make mistakes. In life people often pick a cheaper option. Importantly, often a hospital, charity, state agency, or state legislature has made a form most people use and call the "standard form", and doctors, judges, and other people may not like to follow anything else. This book does provide mostly standard forms.

SOME LESS COMMON OR LESS USEFUL FORMS ARE NOT IN THIS BOOK

This book skips some possible but less common or less useful legal documents.

- A "Codicil" can modify or add to a Will but it is easier and legally safer to just rewrite the whole Will.

- Some people do a "Pet Trust" to help a pet, but it's easier to just give money in Will to person given a pet.

- Some people do a "Revocable Living Trust" so a Trust entity with a Trustee holds property or money during their life, usually done to after death have faster transfer of things and to avoid small delays, costs, or work by others (by "avoiding probate"). But this is rare as it may require moving most of a person's things to a Trust causing maybe years of hassle, mostly to avoid later small work for people happy to be getting things.

- "Childrens Trust" papers can be done so upon a death a Trust gets things for a minor child to manage till 18, but this is rarely done due to possible costs and hassles and since it rarely matters (as this book explains).

- Though separate forms exist usually organ donation in handled in drivers license or state ID paperwork.

NO FEDERAL, MASSACHUSETTS, OR OTHER TAX IS OWED AT A DEATH

Despite what many people think usually no tax is owed due to a death, including no inheritance, estate, or similar taxes. Most people don't need to worry about these taxes.

The "Federal Estate And Gift Tax" is only owed if a tax credit is used up that covers $13.99 million per person in 2025 and later, and this amount increases each year to adjust for inflation.

At the state and local level is a Massachusetts Estate Tax of up to 16%, but it only applies if the dead person had over $2,000,000 of things, and it also doesn't tax anything going to a dead person's spouse.

A few states have taxes that may apply for property there if the owner dies, but they usually don't tax at all if the total is under $3 million.

PROBABLY RE-DO DOCUMENTS IF DIVORCE, MARRY, HAVE CHILD, OR MOVE

Divorcing, marrying, having a new child, or moving to a new state can have big legal effects, and if any of these events occur it is recommended people do a new Will and other Estate Planning papers soon. To help most states say a Will from another state is still valid if people move but this is not always certain.

MOST WILLS HAVE A MISCELLANEOUS PART WITH HELPFUL LANGUAGE

Most Wills have a "Miscellaneous" page with legal language that might help avoid later legal problems.

INFORMATION FORM CAN HELP TELL FAMILY AND FRIENDS THINGS

Many people do some kind of "Information Form" so family or friends after a death know helpful things. People can staple financial records and other pages to this. See form on the next pages to use if wanted.

ESTATE PLANNING HELPFUL INFORMATION

For more space attach copies of form or blank pages. Keep pages by Will or other place for Executor or family.

1. Personal Information (Name, Birthdate, Social Security number, special family details, other):

2. Real estate, vehicles, and other major tangible property (especially if people may not find them):

3. Non-tangible assets like stocks, accounts, investments, loans owed you, and business interests:

4. Possible income or insurance like pensions, retirement, disability, insurance, or contracts:

5. Debts owed by you like credit card, loan, student loan, mortgage, car loans, and accounts payable:

6. Names and information of professionals used (attorneys, accountants, brokers, doctors, others):

7. Computer passwords and helpful files, document places, and safes or safe-deposit boxes code/key:

8. Other helpful things, wishes for funeral, special requests, and last messages to family and friends:

CHAPTER 2
LEGAL TERMS AND BASIC PROPERTY LAW

THERE ARE BASIC LEGAL TERMS AND IDEAS IN ESTATE PLANNING

Some legal terms and ideas are basic to Estate Planning.

■ "Estate Planning" is about people doing legal documents to control things if later absent, sick, or dead. After a document is done people are mostly free to sell or transfer property, instruct doctors, or change forms.

■ A "person doing a legal document" and "doing a form" means the form is for and affects that person.

■ "Probate" is a legal process to do things after someone's death like transfer property, handle creditors, and authorize a Guardian. Due to changes in the law probate is now often informal, faster, and less costly.

■ A "Will" or "will" (this book uses upper case "W") is a legal document done to control issues after death. The phrase "Last Will And Testament" is used since a "Testament" long ago was a small document done along with a Will to do some things.

■ A person doing a Will is called "Testator" or "Will maker". Before about the year 2000 a woman Testator was called a "Testatrix" and woman Executor called an "Executrix" but this is no longer often said or written.

■ If no valid Will is done a person is "intestate" and then a dead person's property and money is transferred to a spouse, children, and family as intestate law says. <u>Some people a fine with this</u>. This is covered later.

■ A person who died is called the "decedent" or "deceased". A person getting a Will gift is called a "recipient", "beneficiary", or "heir" if related (they "inherit"). "Survive" or "surviving" is to be alive after someone else died. The term "descendants" or "issue" usually means a person's children and grandchildren.

■ A person named in a Will to handle things after someone's death is called an "Executor", but if a judge has to pick someone they are called an "Administrator". <u>The new term "Personal Representative" covers both these things and this new term is now commonly used in most Wills in Massachusetts</u>.

■ Legally property is: 1) "real property" which is land and buildings ("real estate"), 2) "fixtures" which are things tied to real property (like fences, carpets, and wired-in appliances), or 3) "personal property" which is everything else (like household items, clothes, tools, cars, jewelry, art, moneys, accounts, and stocks),

■ A person under 18 is usually called a "minor" and often a parent or guardian helps them do things. A minor or other person not reasonably able to make wise decisions lacks "capacity" and is "incapacitated".

■ A document giving power to someone is often called a "Power of Attorney" where the "Principal" gives power to someone called the "Agent" or "Attorney-in-Fact" (but they needn't be a real attorney or a lawyer).

■ State law is the "Massachusetts General Laws" and this has big parts called "Chapters" and each laws is called a "section" or "statute" shown by a "§" symbol. A form found in state law for people to use if they want is called a "statutory form". An example of how to refer to a law is: "Mass. Gen. Laws chapter 81 § 121".

ESTATE MEANS PROPERTY OF DECEDENT AND ENTITY HOLDING THINGS

The "estate" or "probate estate" means <u>all property and money of a dead person</u> that at death or soon after didn't automatically legally go to new owners. Estate is also the <u>name for a temporary entity run by an Executor to do things after a death</u> (it's like a small corporation, e.g., "Estate of John Alan Smith").

PERSON CAN ONLY GIFT IN WILL WHAT THEY OWN AT DEATH

A person can only gift by Will things they own at death, <u>so people should research what they do own</u>. Basically by law a person usually owns all they earn as wages and salary, owns their share of income and profit tied to property they own, and owns or partly owns any things their money buys or improves. And for property with "title" documents (real estate or vehicles) or where there is a "listed owner" (like accounts) the named persons are usually the legal owners unless evidence shows special circumstances. If people don't keep track of how much of their money is in an account shared with a spouse, then the account is usually seen as jointly owned 50/50. Note, a person in life can sell stuff, make gifts, or transfer things, so <u>people should consider if they already sold or gave away property they also name in a Will gift</u>.

NON-PROBATE TRANSFERS THAT HAPPEN AUTOMATICALLY IGNORE A WILL

It is vital to be aware <u>some money or property of a person who dies may automatically transfer on death</u> or soon after to new owners <u>if certain arrangements were made earlier</u>. This is called "non-probate property". Such things transfer as arranged even if a Will names the same items in some Will gifts.

Examples are: a) a "designated beneficiary" form was done to name people to get an investment or account, b) transfer-on-death accounts were used, and c) real property is held by 2 people as "joint tenants with survivorship" or similar so at a death the surviving person gets things. Also, usually property in a Trust will ignore a Will and transfer as Trust papers say to. Life insurance usually goes to the named beneficiary.

Trying to do non-probate transfers for all things is called "avoiding probate", but few people try this since it can cause years of hassle, benefits are small, and often some thing is missed. <u>When doing a Will people should consider non-probate transfers that will occur automatically at a death and consider what will be left</u>.

THINGS OWNED IN SPECIAL WAYS MAY LIMIT GIFTING IN WILL

A person should consider if they own real estate or other property in special ownership ways which may limit gifting by Will. Laws vary in different states but <u>some common special ways of ownership are</u>:

- "joint tenant with right of survivorship" or similar legal options may be used in papers, so at a death property goes automatically to other named owners despite what a Will says (this is often how spouses hold a home);
- papers say a "life estate" exists, so then if someone dies the other people in papers the get a thing; and
- "Trust property" occurs if paperwork made a Trust entity and then property was transferred into it or this is set to occur, so then the Trust papers control where things put in the Trust go after someone's death.

Simple "joint ownership" with many owners can occur if people do joint papers, all agree to it, buy with joint funds, or if a gift was to many people. Wills <u>can</u> gift joint property, like "I give my half of boat to Ed Hu".

CHAPTER 3
WILL BASICS

A WILL LETS A PERSON CONTROL THINGS AFTER THEIR DEATH

A Will is a legal document done by a person to control some things after their death. A person doing a Will is called the "Testator" or "Will maker". In Massachusetts a Testator <u>when signing</u> a Will must be at least age 18, of sound mind (rational with sufficient memory), and not be under duress (unfair pressure or threat).

KEEP SIGNED WILL IN SAFE PLACE IT CAN BE FOUND AFTER A DEATH

A Will should be kept so it can be found within days of a death, like in a desk, drawer, safe, with a person, or rarely a bank safe deposit box. Family can be told how to find a Will. Though rare a person can file a Will at court for safekeeping, and later family or an Executor withdraw it. Mass. Gen. Laws chapter 190B § 2-515.

A WILL MUST BE SIGNED WITH 2 WITNESSES

A WILL TO BE VALID USUALLY MUST BE SIGNED WITH 2 WITNESSES

In Massachusetts a document to be a Will must show it is a Will and a person doing it usually must <u>sign in front of at least 2 persons</u> acting as witnesses who then sign too. A Will just spoken on a video or audio recording usually has no legal effect. Unlike some states Massachusetts does not let witnesses be skipped if a Will is totally handwritten. Some people modify a Will to have 3 or 4 witnesses in case this helps later.

WITNESSES SHOULD BE AT LEAST AGE 18 AND NOT GETTING WILL GIFTS

A person to witness a Will must be at least age 18. Under state law a Will <u>is</u> still valid if a witness or their spouse are getting gifts in the Will, but normally these Will gifts to witnesses are void so won't later be done. The only exceptions are if there are 2 other witnesses to the Will not getting gifts or, alternatively, if somehow it is fully proven that nothing improper led to the gifts or the Will. Mass. Gen. Laws chapter 190B § 2-505. <u>To avoid these issues most people try to pick witnesses who are "disinterested" which means they or their spouse are not getting Will gifts</u>. It is best but not legally required a witness not be old, live far away, or be named in a Will to be Executor, Guardian, or similar job. Usually witnesses are friends, strangers, or family.

TESTATOR AND 2 WITNESSES SIGN THE WILL WHEN TOGETHER IN 1 ROOM

A person doing a Will usually signs it with at 2 witnesses who also sign while all are in 1 room and seeing others sign. A Testator and witnesses should <u>use their full legal name</u> unless they dislike and rarely use it. People showing others an ID is common but not required. Often witnesses print their name and address. Witnesses only read the 1 paragraph of the Will they sign. A Testator need not initial all of the Will pages. Witnesses should be told by someone the document is a Will. Though not required often a Testator says a thing like: "My name is _____ and this is my Will I do voluntarily and ask you 2 people to act as witnesses". Some Testators chat a bit with witnesses about a Will to show they are of sound mind.

MOST WILLS SAY PEOPLE MAY LATER DO INFORMAL PROBATE

Most Wills say after a death the family and friends may do "informal probate" which can avoid costs and delays. Informal probate often is done with just 1 court hearing and often is completed in well under 1 year.

MOST WILLS SAY TO SKIP COSTLY BOND FOR EXECUTOR AND OTHERS

Most Wills helpfully say no "bond" or "surety" is required for any Executor, Guardian, or similar persons. A bond is insurance from a company to insure against misconduct. A Testator usually doesn't want a bond since the persons Testator names are trusted and them later needing a bond will cost the estate money.

OFTEN AT START OF A WILL A PERSON NAMES ANY SPOUSE AND CHILDREN

Many Wills start with a place for a Testator to name any current living spouse and children of any age. Natural or adopted children should be put here including any born outside of marriage. People without this family can skip this or just write "none". Not doing this may invalidate a Will by indicating a person lacks sufficient mental ability, or let a spouse or child not listed ask a judge to give them a share or all of the estate by claiming a Testator forgot them. After listing family in a Will a Testator is often free to give them nothing.

CANCELING OLD WILLS IS USUALLY NOT A PROBLEM

So a new Will is followed old Wills should be canceled ("revoked"). To do this a new Will in the first part usually says old Wills are revoked. Or people can revoke a Will by marking it, like with "void" or a giant "X". Usually crossing out just part of a Will has no effect. Revoking a Will usually doesn't bring back an earlier Will.

A WILL NAMES AN EXECUTOR TO DO THINGS AFTER DEATH

A WILL NAMES SOMEONE TO BE EXECUTOR TO DO THINGS AFTER A DEATH

Usually a Will names someone as "Executor" to act after a death. The law gives Executors many helpful legal powers, like to handle debts, find and collect and give new owners property and money, and do probate If a Will fails to name an Executor a judge can pick someone, but family may argue about who to suggest. Note, the term "Personal Representative" and not Executor is now often used in Massachusetts for a person doing this job after a death, but these terms mostly mean the same thing. Will gifts can go to an Executor.

EXECUTOR CAN BE PAID AND ESTATE PAYS FOR EXECUTOR'S EXPENSES

Massachusetts law says an Executor can ask to can be paid and usually get paid for the hours of work spent, but unlike some other states there is no right to get a percentage of property and money of the estate. For example, an Executor spending 5 hours a week for 40 weeks might ask for $40 an hour and so ask to get paid $8000. But often Executors later skip asking for pay so as to not owe income tax and leave more resources to carry out more Will gifts. Costs any Executor has like for insurance, utilities, repairs, funeral, mortgage, accountants, attorneys, and probate costs are paid for with some money or property of the estate. Any lawyer hired is paid what they and Executor agree on which may be an hourly rate or a fixed sum.

EXECUTOR MUST BE AT LEAST 18 AND SECOND PERSON RARELY IS NEEDED

A person to be Executor must be at least age 18. Massachusetts law does not require a person live here or have no record of crimes or dishonesty, but a judge may later block a person who seems too unsuitable. Naming 2 people to both be Executor is allowed but rare due to the risk of arguments and delays, and since any 1 person named should be trusted. People can name a 2nd fallback person to be Executor just in case the 1st person isn't available but most skip this since this is rare and if needed a judge can pick someone. To add such a 2nd person a person can add: "or if they're reasonably unable to serve I name _____ to serve".

CHAPTER 4
WILL GIFTS INCLUDING RESIDUE CLAUSE

MAIN USE OF A WILL IS TO WRITE GIFTS TO HAPPEN AFTER DEATH

Most people use a Will mainly to legally say what happens to their property and money after their death, usually by writing down various Will gifts to occur when they die. Verbal and even writings about this are not usually valid if not in a written Will. A Will can control property acquired after it was signed. The end of this chapter covers "intestate law" which says where a person's things go at death if no valid Will handles this.

GIFTING IN A WILL USING SIMPLE WORDS OFTEN IS BEST

Making gifts in a Will using simple words is often best, using words like "I give to" and "I gift to". This is legally fine and avoids confusing legal words like "bequest", "devise", and "legacy" which few people know.

A PERSON IS MOSTLY FREE TO GIFT THEIR THINGS AS WANTED

A person is mostly free to give at death their money and property as they want. But creditors a decedent owed money, a spouse, and minor children under age 18 may have some rights which this book later covers.

IN WILL CAN DO SPECIFIC GIFTS TO GIFT PARTICULAR PROPERTY

Most Wills have "specific gifts" to gift particular things. Specific gifts can be any property, like "I give boat to Ed Blom" and "I give UBank account #84553873 to Sue Wu". If a gift is not clear the law assumes all of a kind of thing is given, like "I give jewelry to Ann Po" means all jewelry. But gifting specific property can have surprises like value of items can change, or a Will gift may later fail to occur if property is not owned at death.

IN WILL CAN DO GENERAL GIFTS LIKE OF MONEY

Wills can do "general gifts" where what is gifted is not particular property but can be flexibly chosen, like "I give 1 of my 3 cars to Ed Po" which lets an Executor pick which car. The usual general gift is money, like "I give $5 to Ed Hu". Money gifts are easy to write, let equal gifts be made, and are legally safer for many reasons. To carry out money gifts an Executor usually uses accounts or sells some property in the estate.

GIFT BENEFICIARIES CAN GET PERCENTAGE RATHER THAN EQUAL SHARE

If a Will gift goes to multiple people the law assumes equal shares, but if wanted percentages can be used to make unequal gifts, like "I give boat 90% to John Smith and 10% to Mary Baker".

GIFTS IN WILL CAN GO TO A GROUP OR CLASS OF PEOPLE

To save work a Will gift can go to a group or class of people like certain family if who is meant is later easy to determine. People can say roughly how much in total is gifted to be clearer. Examples are: "I give $10 to each person in my 2018 bowling team" and "I give $10 to each of my grandkids so this is about $100 in total."

PROPERTY OR MONEY IN A JOINT GIFT GOES TO MULTIPLE PEOPLE

The same property or money can go to many people to each get a part, and this is called a "joint gift". For example, "I give boat and all hats to Ann Baxter and Mary Ann Swanson" means each person owns part of every item. People later can split things by agreement or an Executor can decide how to divide items. If a person in a joint gift has died their part usually is left to transfer under a Residue Clause.

RESIDUE CLAUSE IS CATCH-ALL THAT HELPFULLY GIFTS ANYTHING LEFT

This chapter later covers how a Residue Clause at a Will's end gifts property or money not already gifted. Sometimes this is given to a person or their "lineal descendants per stirpes" which means their children and grandchildren with a equal share going to each branch of their family (this is explained later in this book).

GIFT BENEFICIARIES CAN GET PERCENTAGE RATHER THAN EQUAL SHARE

If a Will gift goes to multiple people the law assumes equal shares, but if wanted percentages can be used to make unequal gifts, like "I give boat 90% to John Smith and 10% to Mary Baker".

AFTER A DEATH FAMILIES OFTEN LET PEOPLE TAKE ITEMS UNOFFICIALLY

Many families let people take items <u>unofficially</u> in ways a person said, wrote on notes, or showed by stickers. This often works out fine. If anyone officially objects a judge will have a Will and law be followed, but later people can voluntarily retransfer items. <u>This book later covers how to gift by Tangible Personal Property Memorandum</u>.

CAN LEAVE SOME WILL GIFT AREAS BLANK OR WRITE TO SAY SKIP GIFTS

A person can choose to not use some gifts areas in a Will legal form, like by just leaving areas blank, writing things like "SKIPPED" or "NONE", or using a computer to delete some gift lines. Judges and others usually do not care about neatness or empty spaces in Wills, and will follow whatever parts are filled in.

OPTIONS EXIST TO HANDLE RARE CASE PERSON IN A WILL GIFT DIES

PERSON IN WILL GIFT USUALLY MUST SURVIVE OR GIFT DOES NOT OCCUR

Though rarely an issue, many Wills like this book's Will forms say a person named in a Will gift must survive (live past) the Testator or <u>the gift will not later occur</u> unless gift language specifically says different. If survival isn't required like this then what occurs can be unclear (for many reasons like certain state laws). Most people if they see a person in a gift has died just re-do a Will or trust a Residue Clause to handle it.

SOME PEOPLE ADD "ALTERNATE BENEFICIARY" MAYBE FOR SPECIAL ITEMS

Some people to handle if a person named in a Will gift dies maybe put <u>for special items</u> an alternate beneficiary, like for example: "<u>I give oak table to Ed Wu but if they don't survive me to Ben Fox</u>".

IF PERSON IN GIFT DIES IT CAN GO TO "LINEAL DESCENDANTS PER STIRPES"

A Will gift can say it goes to a person but if they don't survive (outlive) the Testator then say the gift <u>goes to the person's "lineal descendants"</u>. Descendants are a person's children and grandchildren. <u>Importantly, the term "per stirpes" is often used to say to give to each family branch equally</u>. An example shows all this:

> A Will may say: "All clothes to Sue Wu but if they don't survive <u>to their lineal descendants per stirpes</u>", and this means if Sue Wu has died and her son Ken Wu is living and her other son Ben Wu has died but left 2 children then, legally, by law Ken Wu himself gets 50% and Ben Wu's 2 children each get 25%.

HELPFUL LAWS OFTEN REQUIRE PERSON SURVIVE 120 HOURS TO GET GIFT

Laws in most states say a person dying within 120 hours of someone is seen as having died earlier, so often a Will gift to them is ignored. This book's Wills also at the end say this. This avoids legal problems like need to know exact time of death and, also, having an item go through many probate legal cases over years.

RESIDUE CLAUSE GIFTING ANYTHING LEFT IS MAIN WAY TO GIFT THINGS

THE RESIDUE CLAUSE IS A CATCH-ALL THAT GIFTS ANYTHING LEFT

Most Wills by the end have a Residue Clause to give property or money left in a person's estate not gifted earlier in a Will or used other ways. All that is left this way is called the "Residue". Many people let this clause handle most things. This avoids all need to list and describe property and money and also has less legal risk.

USUAL RESIDUE CLAUSE HAS 2 PARTS

A short 2 part Residue Clause is usual and is used in this book's Will forms, and it has:

1) a 1st space to name persons to get things if they survive the Testator (many name a spouse or closest family here), and if several people are named here but only some survive the survivors split things, and

2) a 2nd space to name persons to get things if all in the 1st space don't survive (many people name next closest family or friends here), and if a person in the 2nd space has died their descendants get their share.

EXAMPLE OF 2 PART RESIDUE CLAUSE:

"RESIDUE CLAUSE: The rest, residue, and remainder of my estate, and anything else, I give to:

a) to ____John Doe my husband_____ who survive me and with persons just named who survive me taking the share of non-survivors, then if anything remains

b) to ____Sam Doe, Ann Wu, and Pam Ax_____ and if any of those just named do not survive me their part goes to their lineal descendants per stirpes."

In this example if John Doe has survived he gets everything. If John Doe hasn't survived and also Sam Doe hasn't survived but he left 2 children then, legally, Sam's 2 children split the 1/3 share of his (so get 1/6 each) and the other 2 persons in 2nd part (Ann Wu and Pam Ax) get 1/3 each. Usually the first people named in the clause won't die so gets things, and if they are seen to have died a Will can be redone.

SOME PEOPLE USE PERCENTAGES TO GIFT DIFFERENT AMOUNTS OF RESIDUE

Some people use percentages in a Residue Clause to get the exact split wanted. This can gift a lot (like to a person's children) and gift a small bit (like to a grandchild or more distant people). *See example in Appendix.*

SOME PEOPLE WRITE THE SAME THING IN BOTH PARTS OR SKIP A PART

Some people put the same names in both clause spaces or skip part of it to do certain things. For example, a person with no spouse may skip the 1st part and in 2nd part name their children (including any who died who had kids of their own) so all branches of a person's descendants get a share. *See example in Appendix.*

SOME PEOPLE CHANGE A RESIDUE CLAUSE TO HAVE 1 PART

Some people change a Residue Clause to have just 1 part since this can gift more equally and be easier to understand. *See example in Appendix.* For example a Residue Clause can be made to say:

"The rest, residue, and remainder of my estate, and anything else, I give to: _____ who survive me and if any of those just named do not survive me their part goes to their lineal descendants per stirpes."

MUST SUFFICIENTLY DESCRIBE NAMES AND PROPERTY IN A WILL

PUTTING NAMES OF PEOPLE OR GROUPS IN A WILL IS FAIRLY EASY

Putting names in a Will is fairly easy. Later a judge or Executor assume a person putting names in a Will meant to gift to people they know, so common names are OK unless 2 friends or family use the same name. Details can help if names won't be recognized or to be friendly, like "I give $5 to my nurse Sue Smith" and "I give $5 to loyal pal Ed Dutton". If people mostly used a nickname "also known as" or "a/k/a" may help, like "I give $5 to Dan Smith a/k/a Big Red". Gifts can go to a charity, a government, or a group, like "I give $8 to Goodwill Charities, "I give $8 to the Boston Public Library, Boston, MA", and "I give $8 to Holy Trinity Church of Dallas, Texas". People sometimes phone to learn a charity's or organization's official name.

PUTTING DESCRIPTIONS OF ITEMS IN WILL GIFTS IS FAIRLY EASY

Describing items in gifts is fairly easy. Later a judge or Executor assume a person in a Will meant to gift items they own, and rarely do people own similar things so there is later confusion. Often OK is doing gifts with simple words like: "I give ax to Ed Wu" and "I give big table to Jed Fox". It's OK to gift by category or a list, like: "I give tools to Sam Lee" and "I give cow, van, and harp to Sue Po". For financial items plain words can be used, like "I give bank accounts and stocks to Ann Bima", or details can be used, like: "I give Wells Fargo bank account ending 8714 to Tom Hud". Gifting using a location is riskier as judges will ignore a Will gift if it seems items were placed to affect gifting and for no "independently significant" life reason. So, "I give Ed Po items in my desk and safe" a judge might not follow, but "I give Ed Po hats at cabin" likely is OK.

DESCRIBING REAL PROPERTY IS HARD IF NOT USING RESIDUE OR TITLE

Gifting real property (real estate) and fixtures (things tied to real property like fences, furnaces, and wiring) at death can be hard to do right and the legally safer way to do this is:

a) do nothing specific so it's handled by a Will residue clause, or b) have a lawyer or other person put names in a deed or other document for the real property so then named persons legally get it when the owner dies.

Gifting real property at death a few other ways is legally harder. Helpfully a gift of real property using a location by law gifts all land, buildings, and fixtures located there with no need to list out what's there.

It is possible to gift real property at a particular address with very plain words, like a house, fixtures, and land can be fully given by something like: "I give 86 Maxwell Street, Newton, Massachusetts, to Sue Ann Brown".

People can do a blanket gift giving all of a kind of property, like, "I give all real property and fixtures in Suffolk County, Massachusetts to Ann Ivy Hill " or "I give all real property and fixtures of mine to Eric Paul Carlson".

Giving real property in a Will using a "legal description" is how some lawyers do it, but this can be hard to do. If using a legal description people must write without mistakes the full legal description of maybe many lines into a Will with no abbreviation at all. A legal description might be found on a deed or on mortgage papers. Legal descriptions may refer to a "lot" or "blocks" on a map which is recorded in land records of a county, or it may refer to a path around the land borders with various angles, distances, and iron stakes.

LATER DIVORCE OR MURDER CANCELS WILL GIFTS TO THE ACTING PERSON
If a person divorces or murders a Testator then by state law usually all Will gifts to them are cancelled.

CONDITIONS ON WILL GIFTS ARE RARE DUE TO POSSIBLE PROBLEMS
Putting conditions on a gift, like "I give Ann Poe $90 if she graduates college", can cause problems like years of delay, risk of lawsuits, and big attorney's fees. Due to all this conditions are rarely put on Will gifts.

INTESTATE LAW COVERS PROPERTY OR MONEY NOT HANDLED BY WILL

INTESTATE LAW CONTROLS THINGS NOT HANDLED BY A WILL
Massachusetts "intestate law" says <u>if a person dies with no valid Will</u> or <u>if anything is left after Will and all transfers are done</u> then certain surviving (living) family get property and money left in the person's estate. Many people like what intestate law says and choose to skip a Will, but often doing a Will has some benefit. If somehow property or money is left after following intestate law then it goes to the state of Massachusetts. Note, "descendants" and "issue" both mean a person's children and grandchildren, and if someone dies who would've get an intestate share often their descendants get that share. State intestate law says as follows:

Mass. General Laws chapter 190B § 2–102. [Share of Spouse.]
The intestate share of a decedent's surviving spouse is:
  (1) the entire intestate estate if:
    (i) no descendant or parent of the decedent survives the decedent; or
    (ii) all of the decedent's surviving descendants are also descendants of the surviving spouse and there is no other descendant of the surviving spouse who survives the decedent;
  (2) the first $200,000, plus 3/4 of any balance of the intestate estate, if no descendant of the decedent survives the decedent, but a parent of the decedent survives the decedent;
  (3) the first $100,000 plus 1/2 of any balance of the intestate estate, if all of the decedent's surviving descendants are also descendants of the surviving spouse and the surviving spouse has 1 or more surviving descendants who are not descendants of the decedent;
  (4) the first $100,000 plus 1/2 of any balance of the intestate estate, if 1 or more of the decedent's surviving descendants are not descendants of the surviving spouse.

Mass. General Laws chapter 190B § 2–103. [Share of Heirs Other Than Surviving Spouse.]
<u>Any part of the intestate estate not passing to the decedent's surviving spouse</u> under section 2–102, or the entire intestate estate if there is no surviving spouse, passes in the following order to the individuals designated below who survive the decedent:
  (1) <u>to the decedent's descendants</u> per capita at each generation;
  (2) if there is no surviving descendant, to decedent's parents equally if both survive, or to surviving parent;
  (3) if there is no surviving descendant or parent, to the descendants of the decedent's parents or either of them per capita at each generation;
  (4) if there is [none of the above then equally to the decedent's next of kin in equal degree].

CHAPTER 5
DEBT, HOMESTEAD, MARRIAGE, AND CHILD ISSUES

THIS CHAPTER COVERS CERTAIN ISSUES THAT SOME PEOPLE CAN SKIP
This chapter covers debt, homestead, marriage, and young child issues, and some people can skip parts.

DEBT ISSUES

PAYING DECEDENT'S DEBTS MAY USE UP RESOURCES AND REDUCE GIFTS
If a decedent had debts then creditors owed may ask a judge to be paid from decedent's money or property before Will gifts and certain transfers occur. How debts are paid is set by state law and a Will need not describe this. Funds to pay debts comes from decedent's money and property so may affect (in order) the Will Residue, Will general gifts, Will specific gifts, and non-probate transfers. Probate, health care, taxes, and funeral costs by law have some priority to be paid first. For certain reasons often not all debts are paid. People should consider how paying debts may use up money or property, leaving less to carry out Will gifts. A spouse and family usually aren't liable for decedent's debts unless they actually guaranteed or co-signed.

SECURED DEBTS LIKE MORTGAGE OR VEHICLE LIEN ARE NOT PAID OFF
Laws in most states say do not pay off any secured debts on property of a decedent like a house mortgage or vehicle lien even if other debts are paid by Executor or in probate. This avoids using up estate resources on paying these usually big debts. Due to this, all this book's Will forms say do not usually pay off any secured debts. But if a Testator wants they can 1) put in a Will an order to pay (like, "Executor pay off the house mortgage"), or 2) gift ample enough money to pay off a secured debt to the person getting the property. Most banks let the new owners after a death keep paying monthly any secured debt like a mortgage or lien.

FAMILY RIGHTS MAY BE USED TO GET FAMILY THINGS BEFORE DEBTS
Most states have "Family Rights" a decedent's surviving spouse or children can claim, and this helpfully may let them get things even before most debts of decedent are paid and even before Will gifts.

First, in many U.S. states a decedent's family can use an "Exempt Property" right to get some of decedent's clothing and household items to let family comfortably live. In Massachusetts a spouse (or if there's no spouse the decedent's children) can get $10,000 of decedent's household furniture, vehicles, appliances, and personal effects. Mass. Gen. Laws chapter 190B § 2-403. To the extent possible a family must try to pick items not covered by Will specific gifts. Family can try to get even more by claiming in life decedent gifted them more.

Second, in many U.S. states a decedent's family can use a "Family Allowance" right to some of decedent's money and property to live on a while. Massachusetts has this right and often $2,000 a month during probate or a lump sum of $24,000 is given to a spouse or dependent children. Mass. Gen. Laws ch. 190B § 2-404.

Third, in many U.S. states if a decedent left a small estate the family can use a "Small Estate Affidavit" to get most things without probate or other delay. In Massachusetts a family can do a Small Estate Affidavit to get most things if there is under $25,000 of money and property in a decedent's estate.

So family don't cause legal trouble by using these rights usually a person by Will or other way gives over 50% and any main family house to any spouse or small children. Some people may want to do more research.

HOMESTEAD ISSUES

In many states a surviving spouse or children have some right to get (or just stay in for years) the house or mobile home owned by a decedent under a "Homestead Law". But Massachusetts law mostly does not say family automatically get this. Massachusetts law does say a spouse (or if no spouse then children to age 21) if they somehow will get a house or mobile home from a decedent can protect from creditors either $125,000 of equity or $500,000 of equity if a Declaration Of Homestead was filed by a decedent. But in actual reality usually a person who owns a house or mobile home does papers so any spouse or any children to age 21 will get ownership of the home, including by making them "joint tenants" in papers. Note, so family don't try to cause legal trouble about a house usually a person gives any home to any spouse or young children.

MARRIAGE ISSUES

MASSACHUSETTS USES SEPARATE PROPERTY LAW FOR SPOUSES

Massachusetts like most states uses the Separate Property Law system that says any married person mostly owns their money and property separately and not jointly with a spouse. Due to this a married person is often free to sell during life or gift by Will most of their money or property and not have to involve a spouse. But joint ownership by 2 spouses and not separate ownership can arise in other ways, like by agreement, both spouses paying part of the purchase price, if a gift was to both spouses, or if paperwork calls it joint.

COMMUNITY PROPERTY LAW APPLIES IN OTHER STATES FOR SPOUSES

There are 9 states mostly in the Western U.S. that use the Community Property Law system for married spouses (Arizona, California, Louisiana, Idaho, Nevada, New Mexico, Texas, Washington, and Wisconsin). This system says property or money is owned 50/50 by spouses as Community Property if it comes from mental or physical work while married (like wages or salary) or if items are bought or improved with any other Community Property. People recently moving from these states may face legal issues.

SPOUSE CAN GET ELECTIVE 1/2 OR 1/3 SHARE INSTEAD OF FOLLOWING WILL

A spouse if unhappy with what a Will and other transfers may give them has a right to instead choose (elect) an "Elective Share" of a share of a dead spouse's property and money rather than get what a Will says. To avoid this spouses would have to do a pre-nuptial or similar agreement which is rare. States do this to try to be fair to a spouse. Massachusetts is a bit unique and says the Elective Share if chosen gives a spouse a right to use for life a) 1/3 of decedent's property and money if they left descendants, or b) 1/2 of all this plus $25,000 if they didn't leave descendants. Mass. Gen. Laws ch. 191 § 15. Legally a spouse who abandoned the other without a good excuse may in rare cases not have this right. Note, a spouse instead of the right to use things for life can ask a judge to instead get a 1 time lump sum payment based on the surviving spouse's life expectancy, for example maybe a young spouse can get 1/4 or so of all decedent's things in the estate. In some cases this can cover property or money a decedent gave away or, also, even things not in the estate but held as non-probate property. Clearly if a spouse uses an Elective Share to get 1/4 or other share of the decedent's property and money this may take so much it may interfere with transfers to other people. To avoid a spouse wanting to use the Elective Share most people give over 1/2 of things to any spouse.

CHILD ISSUES

WILL CAN NAME A GUARDIAN TO CARE FOR YOUNG CHILD

If a parent dies with a child under age 18 then any other natural or adopted parent (but not a step-parent) almost always automatically gets control of the child's care (including health care, school, and home issues). This won't occur only if the other parent will be unavailable a long time or is proven unfit in court which is rare. But just in case it is later needed (like later both parents die) a Will often names a healthy and willing relative or friend as "Guardian" to if needed give this care for a child. Some states call this a Guardian of the Person.

WILL CAN NAME A CONSERVATOR TO MANAGE CHILD'S PROPERTY

Since a child until age 18 can't legally easily control property including money a Will often names a person to be "Conservator" to have the job of managing a young child's property and money. Many states call this a Guardian of the Estate. This person decides each year how to use property and money on a child's needs (like on school, health care, and living costs) and then usually at age 18 anything left then goes to the child. A person paying things for a child can ask to be paid back. A judge often holds a yearly hearing to review all spending. As a nice 2nd option to avoid work and costs most Wills say an Executor may name a person including themselves as "Custodian" to manage things under the new Uniform Transfers To Minors Act.

MOST WILLS NAME 1 PERSON TO CARE FOR CHILD AND THEIR PROPERTY

This book's Will forms and most parents name the same 1 person to care for a child and also manage a child's property and money. People can change a Will to name different people for the 2 positions, but this is rarely worth it since parents dying is rare, rarely do children get much, a person smart enough to handle a child often can handle money, and naming different people can lead to arguments and even costly lawsuits between people. Will gifts can go to someone named in a Will to be a Guardian or Conservator.

PERSON TO HELP A CHILD MUST BE AT LEAST 18

To serve in either of these positions and help a child in Massachusetts a person must be at least age 18. Massachusetts law does not require a person live here or have no record of crimes or dishonesty, but a judge may later block a person who seems too unsuitable. The choice by the last living parent is usually followed. If no Will names a person for a position or they're unavailable a judge can pick someone, but family may argue about who to suggest. Naming 2 people to act at the same time in the same position is rare since 2 persons may argue and any 1 person named should be smart enough to act alone. Sometimes the 2 people in a married couple are named for the same position but there can be problems if they later divorce or disagree. Some Wills add a 2nd person to serve if the 1st person named is later not available, like: "or if they are later unable to serve I name _____ to serve"). But most people skip naming a fallback person since it is rarely needed, if a problem is seen a Will can be redone by a person, and a judge can just pick someone if needed.

NAMING PERSONS TO HELP CHILD RARELY MATTERS

A child under 18 having parents die is rare so parents shouldn't worry much about naming people to help. A good U.S. study looked at 72,240 people under age 18 and found only 2014 had lost 1 parent (so 2.78%) and only 97 had lost 2 parents (so a very small 0.13%). *Parent Mortality Census SIPP Paper #288.*

CHAPTER 6
BASIC IDEAS ABOUT HEALTH CARE FORMS

THERE ARE SOME BASIC IDEAS ABOUT HEALTH CARE FORMS
Some ideas help people understand health care forms.

■ By law people controls their own health care by telling medical personnel what they want unless they are "incapacitated" by insufficient ability to a) communicate verbally or by notes, b) be rational, or c) be conscious. Most people keep control of their own care till death or till no big treatment options remain, but some people worry they may be incapacitated a long time so want to do health care forms.

■ Legal documents that help control health care are usually called "Advanced Directives".

■ If an adult 18 or older becomes incapacitated the adult's closest family like spouse or adult child usually can make emergency decisions. But later they usually must then rush to a judge to get further power if no legal document gives them more power over health care.

■ In legal documents a person can be named to have control of health care if needed. This person is often called the "Health Care Agent", "Health Care Attorney-in-Fact", "Health Care Advocate", or a similar name.

■ In legal documents people can write medical instructions doctors, family, and other people must obey.

■ Parents even without legal documents mostly have full power over health care of children under age 18, and the only exception is teens have some freedom to pick their own family planning or gender related care.

■ Some married people do documents to give a spouse power over medical care if they are incapacitated. Some adults especially to age 25 do documents to give this power to parents. The young are less often sick.

■ Pain relief like pain drugs or comfort care is still given even if documents say to stop or limit other care.

■ Most people only do 1 legal document about health care that often names someone to control health care if needed and has a spot for basic instructions (this is sometimes called a "Health Care Power of Attorney").

■ For the rare times stopping health care seems more likely to matter (like due to extreme illness or old age):

-- most people do nothing special and trust family or Health Care Agent to wisely decide when to stop care (they can weigh many factors like pain, cost, likely difficulty of treatment, beliefs, and chances of recovery);

-- a few people do a serious document to say to stop most health care if <u>later</u> doctors think an incapacitated person has very bad health and more medical care likely won't help (sometimes this is called a "Living Will";

-- a few people do a serious document to say <u>starting immediately</u> to not give most medical care (often this is called a "Do-Not-Resuscitate" if about resuscitation, or called a "Physician's Order" if about many treatments).

CHAPTER 7
FORM 1: WILL (STANDARD)

FORM 1 IS A STANDARD WILL THAT IS FLEXIBLE BUT WITHOUT GUARDIANS

Form 1 is a flexible Will that lets a person control many things after their death. This form has no part about a Guardian so is for a person with no child under age 18. A person doing a Will is called a Testator.

THIS FORM IS A WILL WITH SEVERAL PARTS

The form starts with lines for a person to put their name (a full legal name is best but not required) and place of main residence (most put a county but some put a city). The Will is still valid if people later move.

Paragraph 1, "Living Spouse And Children", lets the names of any living spouse and any living children be written (or if there are none skip this or maybe put "none"). This helps show a person is mentally fit and with enough memory to do a Will. Wrongly not listing someone here can let them ask a judge to give them a share or all of a Testator's property and money by claiming they were accidently forgotten.

Paragraph 2, "Gifts", has many spaces to make some specific gifts of particular property or some general gifts like of money. People can delete, copy and paste to add more, or leave blank these gift lines.

Paragraph 3, "Separate Writings", says to follow any separate writings done at a later time apart from the Will that gifts tangible personal property (see earlier part of this book explaining such a writing).

Paragraph 4, "Residue", has a Residue Clause to say any property and money left after earlier Will parts and other transfers is to be distributed in the way a person wrote in the blank parts of this paragraph.

Paragraph 5, "Administration", names a person to be Personal Representative to do things after a person's death (in the past the term Executor was usually used in Massachusetts for the person doing this).

Paragraph 6, "Miscellaneous", has paragraphs of legal language to help avoid certain legal issues.

Last is a paragraph for Testator to put the date and sign, and a paragraph for 2 witnesses to put the date, sign, and print the addresses they live at.

USUAL RESIDUE CLAUSE HAS 2 PLACES TO NAME PERSONS TO GET THINGS

In a Will "Residue Clause" anything left over after other Will parts is transferred as the clause directs. Many people use a Residue Clause to gift most their things. In this Will form's Residue Clause there is:

1) a 1st space to name 1 or more persons to get the Residue, and if any named here have died before the Will maker then other persons named here in this 1st space take the dead person's share, and

2) a 2nd space to name people to get things if all people named in the 1st space have died, and if any people named in the 2nd space have died their shares go to "lineal descendants" like their children.

People often put in the 1st space a spouse or closest family or friends, and in 2nd space next closest people.

TESTATOR AND 2 WITNESSES WHILE TOGETHER SIGN WILL

This Will after being filled out (except bits intentionally left blank) must be signed by the person doing the Will (the "Testator") in front of at least 2 persons acting as witnesses at least age 18 who then also sign.

LAST WILL AND TESTAMENT

I, _____, of _____, Massachusetts, do revoke all prior Wills and testamentary documents and do make, publish, and declare this as my Will. I am of sound mind and under no duress or undue influence and act voluntarily.

1. LIVING SPOUSE AND CHILDREN. To show I am mentally fit and have sufficient memory to do a Will I do say I now have the following living spouse and living children:
_____
_____.

2. GIFTS. I give these gifts in this Will, but to get a gift in this section the recipient must survive me except as otherwise stated below.

I give _____ to _____.
I give _____ to _____.
I give _____ to _____.
I give _____ to _____.
I give _____ to _____.
I give _____ to _____.
I give _____ to _____.
I give _____ to _____.

3. SEPARATE WRITINGS. I may do writings separate from this Will to gift tangible personal property as allowed by state law, and all such writings should be followed. But any such writing not found within 90 days of my death is canceled and has no effect. A gift in such a writing to a person who does not survive me is canceled and has no effect. This Will does not revoke any such writings that now exist.

4. RESIDUE. The rest, residue, and remainder of my estate, and anything else, I give:
   a) to _____ who survive me, and with persons just named who survive me taking the share of non-survivors, then if anything remains
   b) to _____ and if any of those just now named do not survive me their part goes to their lineal descendants per stirpes.

5. ADMINISTRATION. I name, nominate, and appoint _____ as Personal Representative including for me, my Will, and my estate.

6. MISCELLANEOUS. The following applies to this Will and generally.

In this Will no part left unfilled is a mistake including spaces in the residue clause.

The facts support and I want Massachusetts state law to apply to this Will and my estate. The term state and references to this include the Commonwealth of Massachusetts.

I order that my just debts, funeral and related expenses, and taxes be paid as soon after my death as practical but only those items my Personal Representative chooses to pay.

Priority of Will gifts of the same type is based on the order they are made in this Will.

The words give and gift also means a devise, bequest, grant, legacy, or similar.

I am intentionally not providing by Will or other ways for some family, including I am not providing for some children of mine and also children of a deceased child of mine.

If a Will gift reasonably mentions survival then survival is an absolute condition and anti-lapse laws or similar provisions have no effect and without survival the gift lapses. Unless a Will gift specifies otherwise if a Will gift goes to multiple recipients if any do not survive me the part to them lapses and instead goes to other surviving recipients.

No earlier transfer reduces a Will gift unless I usually called it a loan or advancement.

In this Will any gendered word includes all genders, and the singular includes the plural and vice versa, and they can mean a single person or many persons.

Unless a Will specifically says otherwise a secured debt including a mortgage or lien shall not be paid off including by a Personal Representative or in probate, and a recipient of a Will gift of property takes it subject to debts. Also, no recipient of property who may lose it or who pays to keep it may have my estate or others pay or do exoneration.

If I somehow lost ownership of an item in a specific Will gift the gift is extinguished.

I request and authorize any informal, summary, and quick probate or similar action. Any Personal Representative may act independently with no supervision of any court, including independent administration, and with no inventory, appraisal, or other action.

I give any Personal Representative the a) fullest authority, discretion, and powers allowed by state law, b) power to lease, sell, mortgage, convey, or keep property including real property in a manner and time they deem helpful or proper, and c) authority to settle or pay claims or debts in the time and manner they choose.   Any Personal Representative or other fiduciary shall have all powers and authorities that may be given by statute or common law in any jurisdiction they may act, including under Massachusetts law.

Any Guardian of any type, Conservator, Custodian, or other person managing a minor's property or money may use or invade the principal and sell property without court action.

If context permits the terms Personal Representative and Executor and Administrator are interchangeable, Conservator and Guardian of the Estate and Guardian of Property and Custodian are interchangeable, and residue and residuary are interchangeable. Any such person may stand in the place of and have all powers like the others named here.

The residue includes lapsed or failed gifts, insurance paid to the estate, digital assets, inheritances owed me, and all I had power of appointment or testamentary disposition over.

Any Personal Representative may access, manage, delete, modify, transfer, and

otherwise control any digital accounts and assets I had any interest in or power over.

Any Personal Representative, Executor, Administrator, Guardian of any type like for a person or estate, Conservator, Custodian, and any other fiduciary under this Will or otherwise shall qualify and serve without bond, surety, security, surety bond, or similar.

If evidence does not show it likely a person survived me by 120 hours (5 days) then for this Will and my estate they shall be deemed in all ways as having died before me.

If part of this Will is by law invalid or unenforceable other provisions remain in effect.

Any Personal Representative may at any time transfer money or property of a minor under age 18 to a Custodian to serve under the Massachusetts Uniform Transfers to Minors Act or similar law anywhere, and may pick a person to be Custodian including themselves.

TESTATOR

In witness whereof, I, _____, the Testator, sign my name to this instrument this _____ day of _____, 20_____, and being first duly sworn, do hereby declare to the undersigned authority that I sign and execute this instrument as my Will and that I sign it willingly, that I execute it as my free and voluntary act for the purposes therein expressed, and that I am 18 years of age or older, of sound mind, and under no constraint or undue influence.

_____
Signature of Testator

WITNESSES

We, _____ and _____, Witnesses, sign our names to this instrument, being first duly sworn, and we do hereby declare to the undersigned authority that the Testator signs and executes this instrument as the Testator's Will and that the Testator signs it willingly, and that each of us in the presence and hearing of the Testator hereby signs this Will to do the act of witnessing the Testator's signing, and that to the best of our knowledge the Testator is 18 years of age or older, of sound mind, and under no constraint or undue influence.

_____   _____
Signature of Witness #1   Address of Witness #1

_____   _____
Signature of Witness #2   Address of Witness #2

CHAPTER 8
FORM 2: WILL (GUARDIAN)

FORM 2 IS A WILL WITH GUARDIAN PART FOR PEOPLE WITH YOUNG CHILD
Form 2 is a Will with a Guardian part to be used by a person with a minor child under age 18.

FORM IS A WILL WITH SEVERAL PARTS INCLUDING A GUARDIAN PART
The form starts with lines for a person to put their name (a full legal name is best but not required) and place of main residence (most put a county but some put a city). The Will is still valid if people later move.

Paragraph 1, "Living Spouse And Children", lets names of any living spouse and any living children be written (or if there are none skip this or maybe put "none"). This helps show a person is mentally fit and with enough memory to do a Will. Wrongly not listing someone here can sometimes cause legal problems.

Paragraph 2, "Gifts", has many spaces to make some specific gifts of particular property or some general gifts like of money. People can delete, copy and paste to add more, or leave blank these gift lines.

Paragraph 3, "Separate Writings", says to follow any separate writings done at a later time apart from the Will that gifts tangible personal property (see earlier part of this book explaining such a writing).

Paragraph 4, "Residue", has a Residue Clause to say any property and money left after earlier Will parts and other transfers is to be distributed in the way a person wrote in the blank parts of this paragraph.

Paragraph 5, "Administration", names a person to be Personal Representative to do things after a person's death (in the past the term Executor was usually used in Massachusetts for the person doing this).

<u>**Paragraph 6, "Guardian"**, names a person as Guardian to care for minor children under 18 if needed (like if both parents die) and also as Conservator to manage property and money of children.</u>

Paragraph 7, "Miscellaneous", has paragraphs of legal language to help avoid certain legal issues.

Last is a paragraph for Testator to put the date and sign, and a paragraph for 2 witnesses to put the date, sign, and print the addresses they live at.

USUAL RESIDUE CLAUSE HAS 2 PLACES TO NAME PERSONS TO GET THINGS
In a Will "Residue Clause" anything left over after other Will parts is transferred as the clause directs. Many people use a Residue Clause to gift most their things. In this Will form's Residue Clause there is:
 1) a 1st space to name 1 or more persons to get the Residue, and if any named here have died before the Will maker then other persons named here in this 1st space take the dead person's share, and
 2) a 2nd space to name people to get things if all people named in the 1st space have died, and if any people named in the 2nd space have died their shares go to "lineal descendants" like their children.

People often put in the 1st space a spouse or closest family or friends, and in 2nd space next closest people.

TESTATOR AND 2 WITNESSES WHILE TOGETHER SIGN WILL
This Will after being filled out (except bits intentionally left blank) must be signed by the person doing the Will (the "Testator") in front of at least 2 persons acting as witnesses at least age 18 who then also sign.

LAST WILL AND TESTAMENT

I, _____, of _____, Massachusetts, do revoke all prior Wills and testamentary documents and do make, publish, and declare this as my Will. I am of sound mind and under no duress or undue influence and act voluntarily.

1. LIVING SPOUSE AND CHILDREN. To show I am mentally fit and have sufficient memory to do a Will I do say I now have the following living spouse and living children:
_____
_____.

2. GIFTS. I give these gifts in this Will, but to get a gift in this section the recipient must survive me except as otherwise stated below.

I give _____ to _____.
I give _____ to _____.
I give _____ to _____.
I give _____ to _____.
I give _____ to _____.
I give _____ to _____.
I give _____ to _____.
I give _____ to _____.

3. SEPARATE WRITINGS. I may do writings separate from this Will to gift tangible personal property as allowed by state law, and all such writings should be followed. But any such writing not found within 90 days of my death is canceled and has no effect. A gift in such a writing to a person who does not survive me is canceled and has no effect. This Will does not revoke any such writings that now exist.

4. RESIDUE. The rest, residue, and remainder of my estate, and anything else, I give:
   a) to _____ who survive me, and with persons just named who survive me taking the share of non-survivors, then if anything remains
   b) to _____ and if any of those just now named do not survive me their part goes to their lineal descendants per stirpes.

5. ADMINISTRATION. I name, nominate, and appoint _____ as Personal Representative including for me, my Will, and my estate.

6. GUARDIAN. I name, nominate, and appoint _____
to be Guardian of any minor child of mine and to have care, authority, custody, and other control of them (including as Guardian of the Person). I name this same person to be Conservator for any minor child and to have care, control, and power over their property, money, and estate (including as Guardian of the Estate).

7. MISCELLANEOUS. The following applies to this Will and generally.

    In this Will no part left unfilled is a mistake including spaces in the residue clause.

    The facts support and I want Massachusetts state law to apply to this Will and my estate. The term state and references to this include the Commonwealth of Massachusetts.

    I order that my just debts, funeral and related expenses, and taxes be paid as soon after my death as practical but only those items my Personal Representative chooses to pay.

    Priority of Will gifts of the same type is based on the order they are made in this Will.

    The words give and gift also means a devise, bequest, grant, legacy, or similar.

    I am intentionally not providing by Will or other ways for some family, including I am not providing for some children of mine and also children of a deceased child of mine.

    If a Will gift reasonably mentions survival then survival is an absolute condition and anti-lapse laws or similar provisions have no effect and without survival the gift lapses. Unless a Will gift specifies otherwise if a Will gift goes to multiple recipients if any do not survive me the part to them lapses and instead goes to other surviving recipients.

    No earlier transfer reduces a Will gift unless I usually called it a loan or advancement.

    In this Will any gendered word includes all genders, and the singular includes the plural and vice versa, and they can mean a single person or many persons.

    Unless a Will specifically says otherwise a secured debt including a mortgage or lien shall not be paid off including by a Personal Representative or in probate, and a recipient of a Will gift of property takes it subject to debts. Also, no recipient of property who may lose it or who pays to keep it may have my estate or others pay or do exoneration.

    If I somehow lost ownership of an item in a specific Will gift the gift is extinguished.

    I request and authorize any informal, summary, and quick probate or similar action. Any Personal Representative may act independently with no supervision of any court, including independent administration, and with no inventory, appraisal, or other action.

    I give any Personal Representative the a) fullest authority, discretion, and powers allowed by state law, b) power to lease, sell, mortgage, convey, or keep property including real property in a manner and time they deem helpful or proper, and c) authority to settle or pay claims or debts in the time and manner they choose. Any Personal Representative or other fiduciary shall have all powers and authorities that may be given by statute or common law in any jurisdiction they may act, including under Massachusetts law.

    Any Guardian of any type, Conservator, Custodian, or other person managing a minor's property or money may use or invade the principal and sell property without court action.

    If context permits the terms Personal Representative and Executor and Administrator are interchangeable, Conservator and Guardian of the Estate and Guardian of Property and

Custodian are interchangeable, and residue and residuary are interchangeable. Any such person may stand in the place of and have all powers like the others named here.

The residue includes lapsed or failed gifts, insurance paid to the estate, digital assets, inheritances owed me, and all I had power of appointment or testamentary disposition over.

Any Personal Representative may access, manage, delete, modify, transfer, and otherwise control any digital accounts and assets I had any interest in or power over.

Any Personal Representative, Executor, Administrator, Guardian of any type like for a person or estate, Conservator, Custodian, and any other fiduciary under this Will or otherwise shall qualify and serve without bond, surety, security, surety bond, or similar.

If evidence does not show it likely a person survived me by 120 hours (5 days) then for this Will and my estate they shall be deemed in all ways as having died before me.

If part of this Will is by law invalid or unenforceable other provisions remain in effect.

Any Personal Representative may at any time transfer money or property of a minor under age 18 to a Custodian to serve under the Massachusetts Uniform Transfers to Minors Act or similar law anywhere, and may pick a person to be Custodian including themselves.

TESTATOR

In witness whereof, I, _____, the Testator, sign my name to this instrument this _____ day of _____, 20_____, and being first duly sworn, do hereby declare to the undersigned authority that I sign and execute this instrument as my Will and that I sign it willingly, that I execute it as my free and voluntary act for the purposes therein expressed, and that I am 18 years of age or older, of sound mind, and under no constraint or undue influence.

_____
Signature of Testator

WITNESSES

We, _____ and _____, Witnesses, sign our names to this instrument, being first duly sworn, and we do hereby declare to the undersigned authority that the Testator signs and executes this instrument as the Testator's Will and that the Testator signs it willingly, and that each of us in the presence and hearing of the Testator hereby signs this Will to do the act of witnessing the Testator's signing, and that to the best of our knowledge the Testator is 18 years of age or older, of sound mind, and under no constraint or undue influence.

_____   _____
Signature of Witness #1   Address of Witness #1

_____   _____
Signature of Witness #2   Address of Witness #2

CHAPTER 9
FORM 3: SELF-PROVING AFFIDAVIT

FORM CAN BE DONE TO HELP WITH THE WORK OF USING A WILL LATER

This form is optional but can be done right after a Will is done, or anytime afterward, to help with the legal work that is involved in later using a Will after a death. This form is a statutory form that is found in Massachusetts law.

FORM HELPS SHOW A WILL WAS PROPERLY SIGNED

The Self-Proving Affidavit helps "prove" a Will was signed properly. If this form isn't done then after a death a little more work is needed to get evidence from witnesses to the Will signing, persons familiar with the signatures of people, or a handwriting expert. Without the Self-Proving Affidavit there is a bit more legal risk a Will won't be followed later. But of people doing Wills about half skip a Self-Proving Affidavit mostly due to the hassle of finding a notary on top of 2 witnesses each time a Will is done, and since it requires work of someone mostly to save later work by people who will be happy to be getting things in the Will.

FORM IS DONE BY TESTATOR AND 2 WITNESSES SIGNING BEFORE NOTARY

For this form to be valid a person who is a notary (also called a "notary public") must see the Testator and 2 witnesses sign this form and then the notary notarizes the form. A notary can be found and asked to help at a bank, insurance agent, government office, or by first using a phonebook. This form is often done a few minutes after a Will is signed but it also can be done later (even years later) when everyone can meet with a notary. But this form can't be done before a Will is done. This form when it is completed is often kept paper-clipped to the Will it supports.

SELF-PROVING AFFIDAVIT

(Mass. Gen. Laws chapter 190B section 2-504)

THE STATE OF MASSACHUSETTS
COUNTY OF _____

We, _____, _____, and _____, the Testator and the Witnesses, respectively, whose names are signed to the attached or foregoing instrument, being first duly sworn, do hereby declare to the undersigned authority that the Testator signed and executed the instrument as the Testator's Will and that the Testator had signed willingly, and that the Testator executed it as the Testator's free and voluntary act for the purposes therein expressed, and that each of the Witnesses, in the presence and hearing of the Testator, signed the Will to act as a witness and that to the best of the knowledge of each Witness the Testator was at that time 18 years of age or older, of sound mind, and under no constraint or undue influence.

_____
Testator

_____   _____
Witness   Witness

Subscribed, sworn to and acknowledged before me by , the testator, and subscribed and sworn to before me by _____ and _____, the Witnesses, this _____ day of _____, 20_____.

(Seal)

Signed: _____

Official capacity of officer: _____

CHAPTER 10
FORM 4: TANGIBLE PERSONAL PROPERTY MEMORANDUM

FORM LETS MORE GIFTS TO OCCUR AFTER DEATH BE EASILY WRITTEN OUT
This form lets more gifts to occur after death be easily written, but it can only cover tangible personal property. Many people call this a memo or list form.

FORM GIVES EASY AND QUICK WAY TO WRITE MORE GIFTS OF PROPERTY
This form lets people write out gifts of property to occur after death without any need to re-do a Will or modify a Will. To use this form a valid Will must have been done saying these writings can be used, and most Wills in the state say this (including Wills in this book). If this form and a Will cover the same item then legally the Will later controls what happens. If 2 of these forms cover the same item then the more recently done page controls. People can modify or add to an existing form page if they add a new date and signature. Doing gifts by putting stickers or notes on items is not recommended or legal, and it is better to use this form. To avoid delay the form says to ignore the form if it isn't found within 90 days of a death.

FORM CAN ONLY GIFT TANGIBLE PERSONAL PROPERTY
By law the form can only gift "tangible personal property". This is property that is tangible (touchable), so not accounts, not moneys, and not investments where ownership involves papers or a bank or other entity. This is property that is personal property, so not real property (land or buildings) and not fixtures (anything tied to land) and not money. The form also can't gift any money, whether coin or paper currency, and no matter how old or foreign. Most lawyers recommend the form not be used to gift property used in a business. Improper property written in the form is later just ignored. This form is often used to gift clothes, furniture, cars, boats, antiques, electronics, appliances, tools, building supplies, art, and jewelry.

It may help to see the law allowing the form, Mass. Gen. Laws chapter 190B Section 2-513, which says:

Section 2-513. Separate Writing Identifying Devise of Certain Types of Tangible Property.

A Will may refer to a written statement or list to dispose of items of tangible personal property not otherwise specifically disposed of by the will, other than money.

To be admissible under this section as evidence of the intended disposition, the writing shall be signed by the testator and shall describe the items and the devisees with reasonable certainty.

The writing may be referred to as one to be in existence at the time of the testator's death; it may be prepared before or after the execution of the Will; it may be altered by the testator after its preparation; and it may be a writing that has no significance apart from its effect on the dispositions made by the Will.

TO COMPLETE THE FORM A PERSON SIGNS AND DATES IT
The form must be signed and usually dated, and no witnesses are needed. Pages of this form are often kept by a Will. To cancel this form it can be destroyed, crossed out, or just thrown away so it isn't found later.

TANGIBLE PERSONAL PROPERTY MEMORANDUM

In this writing are gifts of tangible personal property to occur at my death, but this writing if not found by someone within 90 days of my death is canceled.

I may do many pages of these writings which should all be seen as one document. If there are conflicts among such writings the provisions of the more recent writing will revoke the inconsistent provisions of a prior writing.

If a person getting a gift below does not survive me such gift is void and canceled.

DESCRIPTION OF PROPERTY		NAME OF PERSONS TO GET PROPERTY
_____	to	_____
_____	to	_____
_____	to	_____
_____	to	_____
_____	to	_____
_____	to	_____
_____	to	_____
_____	to	_____
_____	to	_____
_____	to	_____
_____	to	_____
_____	to	_____
_____	to	_____
_____	to	_____
_____	to	_____
_____	to	_____
_____	to	_____
_____	to	_____
_____	to	_____

DATE:_____ **SIGNED:**_____

CHAPTER 11
FORM 5: HEALTH CARE PROXY

FORM CAN NAME HEALTH CARE AGENT AND GIVE INSTRUCTIONS

This form lets a person name someone to make health care decisions if needed and also write health care instructions. This book's form is a form written by several hospitals which many people here use. Many people do just this 1 health care form. This form only matters if later a person is incapacitated due to an inability to stay conscious, communicate, or be rational.

CAN NAME HEALTH CARE AGENT TO HAVE POWER OVER HEALTH CARE

This form <u>lets a "Health Care Agent" be named</u> to have power to make medical decisions if a person is later incapacitated. Often named is a spouse, adult child, relative, or friend. Naming a family member as the Agent can avoid their need to rush to see a judge to get more power in an emergency. A person's doctor or anyone working at a place giving health care can't be the Agent unless they are also family. The form has a spot to name an "Alternate Agent" to serve if the first person is unavailable but many people do not bother with this. <u>In the form instructions or limitations</u> on the Agent can be written, but most people skip this since they trust the Agent and it is hard to write clear instructions that don't risk a legal problem.

LIVING WILL SAYING THAT LATER ALL CARE SHOULD STOP IS NOT USED

Massachusetts is one of a few states that does <u>not</u> let a person write to say stop most health care if <u>later</u> doctors think more care is unlikely to help. This is a "Living Will" since it's followed while a person is living. This subject is often called "end-of-life" issues. In Massachusetts for end-of-life issues a person can just <u>give instructions to family or Health Care Agent in some writing or verbally and hope it's followed</u>, for example: "I don't want medical care only likely to prolong life and not get me healthy, and I want care for comfort and limit pain even if it shortens my life". Or <u>a person can do a legal form asking about end-of-life "wishes" or "preferences"</u> which is not legally binding but hopefully family and others will follow what is says to do. Such a form is at www.honoringchoicesmass.com/personal-directive. These end-of-life issues rarely come up and <u>most people do nothing</u> and trust their family and Health Care Agent to handle things if needed.

THIS BOOK COVERS SAYING TO IMMEDIATELY NO LONGER GIVE CARE

Though <u>rarely</u> done this book's next chapter says how a person can use separate legal documents to let a person say <u>immediately</u> no longer try resuscitation like C.P.R. and also most medical treatments.

SIGN FORM WITH 2 WITNESSES

To do the Health Care Proxy a person signs it when in front of 2 witnesses and then the witnesses sign. The persons who are witnesses must be at least age 18 and can't be named Agent. The form sometimes is quickly shown to any doctor or facility that may give health care. A person can keep the signed form until needed or can hand it to the Agent or family members to hold. To cancel the form a person can tell the Agent and maybe also any doctor or place that saw the form that it is canceled.

YOUR BIRTH DATE (m/d/y)
____/____/____

MASSACHUSETTS HEALTH CARE PROXY

1 I, _____, residing at
(Principal: PRINT your name)

_____
(Street)   (City/town)   (State/ZIP)

appoint as my **Health Care Agent**: _____
(Name of person you choose as Agent)

of _____
(Street)   (City/town)   (State/ZIP)

Agent's tel (h) _____ (w) _____ E-mail _____

OPTIONAL: If my agent is unwilling or unable to serve, then I appoint as my **Alternate Agent**:

_____
(Name of person you choose as Alternate Agent)

of _____
(Street)   (City/town)   (State/ZIP)   (Phone)

2 My Agent shall have the authority to make all health care decisions for me, including decisions about life-sustaining treatment, subject to any limitations I state below, if I am unable to make health care decisions myself. My Agent's authority becomes effective if my attending physician determines in writing that I lack the capacity to make or to communicate health care decisions. My Agent is then to have the same authority to make health care decisions as I would if I had the capacity to make them **EXCEPT** (here list the limitations, *if any*, you wish to place on your Agent's authority):

I direct my Agent to make health care decisions based on my Agent's assessment of my personal wishes. If my personal wishes are unknown, my Agent is to make health care decisions based on my Agent's assessment of my best interests. Photocopies of this Health Care Proxy shall have the same force and effect as the original and may be given to other health care providers.

3   **Signed**:_____ **Date**: ___/___/___ (mo/day/yr)

Complete only if Principal is physically unable to sign: I have signed the Principal's name above at his/her direction in the presence of the Principal and two witnesses.

_____   _____
(Name)   (Street)

                                        _____
                                        (City/town)   (State/ZIP)

4   **WITNESS STATEMENT:** We, the undersigned, each witnessed the signing of this Health Care Proxy by the Principal or at the direction of the Principal and state that the Principal appears to be at least 18 years of age, of sound mind and under no constraint or undue influence. Neither of us is named as the Health Care Agent or Alternate Agent in this document.
In our presence, on this day ___/___/___ (mo / day / yr).

Witness #1 _____   Witness #2 _____
                (Signature)   (Signature)

Name (print) _____   Name (print) _____

Address _____   Address _____

5   Statements of Health Care Agent and Alternate Agent (OPTIONAL)

Health Care Agent: I have been named by the Principal as the Principal's **Health Care Agent** by this Health Care Proxy. I have read this document carefully, and have personally discussed with the Principal his/her health care wishes at a time of possible incapacity. I know the Principal and accept this appointment freely. I am not an operator, administrator or employee of a hospital, clinic, nursing home, rest home, Soldiers Home or other health facility where the Principal is presently a patient or resident or has applied for admission. But if I am a person so described, I am also related to the Principal by blood, marriage, or adoption. If called upon and to the best of my ability, I will try to carry out the Principal's wishes.

(Signature of **Health Care Agent**)_____

Alternate Agent: I have been named by the Principal as the Principal's **Alternate Agent** by this Health Care Proxy. I have read this document carefully, and have personally discussed with the Principal his/her health care wishes at a time of possible incapacity. I know the Principal and accept this appointment freely. I am not an operator, administrator or employee of a hospital, clinic, nursing home, rest home, Soldiers Home or other health facility where the Principal is presently a patient or resident or has applied for admission. But if I am a person so described, I am also related to the Principal by blood, marriage, or adoption. If called upon and to the best of my ability, I will try to carry out the Principal's wishes.

(Signature of **Alternate Agent**)_____

*   *   *   *   *

Health Care Proxy developed by Massachusetts Health Decisions in association with the following member organizations of the Massachusetts Health Care Proxy Task Force:

Boston University Schools of Medicine and Public Health: Law, Medicine, and Ethics Program	Massachusetts Hospital Association
	Massachusetts Medical Society
Deaconess ElderCare Program	Massachusetts Nurses Association
Hospice Federation of Massachusetts	Medical Center of Central Massachusetts
Massachusetts Bar Association	Suffolk University Law School: Elder Law Clinic
Massachusetts Department of Public Health	
Massachusetts Executive Office of Elder Affairs	University of Massachusetts at Boston: The Gerontology Institute
Massachusetts Federation of Nursing Homes	
Massachusetts Health Decisions	Visiting Nurse Associations of Massachusetts

Additional information and resources for individuals, organizations and professionals available at **https://masshealthdecisions.org**. Or email: **proxy@masshealthdecisions.org**

Massachusetts Health Decisions

CHAPTER 12
FORM 6: DO NOT RESUSCITATE

IN FORM CAN IMMEDIATELY REFUSE MOST HEALTH CARE

This chapter actually has 2 forms which are similar and people pick from to do the serious act of saying to immediately no longer try certain or most health care. Doing this is serious and often only the sickest or oldest people do it. Both forms are often called the "Do Not Resuscitate" or "DNR" form. Both forms are official state forms. Both forms are short and usually will be followed by paramedics and similar personnel.

FIRST FORM SAYS TO IMMEDIATELY NOT GIVE MANY KINDS OF CARE

This chapter's first form, the "Massachusetts Medical Orders For Life-Sustaining Treatment" form (often called the M.O.L.S.T. form), says to immediately not give the many kinds of health care named in it. This form can say to immediately no longer try C.P.R., antibiotics, and artificial feeding. This form is short so it can be read fast and be followed by those in a hurry like paramedics outside a health facility, but this form is more often used by people who are in a care facility. Pain relief and comfort care is usually still given, so paramedics are still usually called if needed to get this. After doing this form a person is usually still free to verbally override it, like by saying a person changed their mind and want all care to a paramedic or doctor. In recent years the M.O.L.S.T. form has become the usual form used to say to immediately no longer try certain health care, and other forms are less often used including this chapter's second form.

SECOND FORM SAYS TO IMMEDIATELY NOT TRY RESUSCITATION

This chapter's second form, the "Do Not Resuscitate" form (often called the D-N-R form) says to now immediately not give any more resuscitation, which is trying to restart or help with breathing or the heart. Resuscitation covers cardio-pulmonary resuscitation (C.P.R.), defibrillation (electric shocks), and machine or tube breathing. This form is short so it can be read fast and followed by those in a hurry like paramedics, and this form is more often used by people outside and not inside a care facility. Pain relief and comfort care is usually still given, so paramedics are still usually called if needed. Note, even after doing form a person is usually free to verbally override it, like by saying to a paramedic or doctor to give all care. Some people also choose to wear a special D-N-R bracelet made by companies chosen by the state that doctors can help get.

FORM IS SIGNED BY DOCTOR OR SIMILAR AND THEN THE PATIENT

To be valid form these forms must be signed by a person's doctor (physician) or other similar health professional, and by the person doing the form (or their named representative who is authorized to do this). Once the form is done people usually people show it to all places that may give care to add it medical files so it is followed. Usually the person also keeps a copy of the form near their body to show to paramedics or similar personnel who may try to give health care.

MASSACHUSETTS MEDICAL ORDERS for LIFE-SUSTAINING TREATMENT

(MOLST) www.molst-ma.org

Patient's Name _____

Date of Birth _____

Medical Record Number if applicable: _____

INSTRUCTIONS: *Every patient should receive full attention to comfort.*

→ This form should be signed based on goals of care discussions between the patient (or patient's representative signing below) and the signing clinician.
→ Sections A–C are valid orders only if Sections D and E are complete. Section F is valid only if Sections G and H are complete.
→ If any section is not completed, there is no limitation on the treatment indicated in that section.
→ The form is effective immediately upon signature. Photocopy, fax or electronic copies of properly signed MOLST forms are valid.

A Mark one circle	**CARDIOPULMONARY RESUSCITATION: for a patient in cardiac or respiratory arrest**	
	O Do Not Resuscitate	O Attempt Resuscitation
B Mark one circle	**VENTILATION: for a patient in respiratory distress**	
	O Do Not Intubate and Ventilate	O Intubate and Ventilate
Mark one circle	O Do Not Use Non-invasive Ventilation (e.g. CPAP)	O Use Non-invasive Ventilation (e.g. CPAP)
C Mark one circle	**TRANSFER TO HOSPITAL**	
	O Do Not Transfer to Hospital (*unless needed for comfort*)	O Transfer to Hospital
PATIENT or patient's representative signature **D** *Required* Mark one circle and fill in every line for valid Page 1.	**Mark one circle below to indicate who is signing Section D:** o Patient o Health Care Agent o Guardian* o Parent/Guardian* of minor Signature of patient confirms this form was signed of patient's own free will and reflects his/her wishes and goals of care as expressed to the Section E signer. Signature by the patient's representative (indicated above) confirms that this form reflects his/her assessment of the patient's wishes and goals of care, or if those wishes are unknown, his/her assessment of the patient's best interests. **A guardian can sign only to the extent permitted by MA law. Consult legal counsel with questions about a guardian's authority.* X_____ _____ Signature of Patient (or Person Representing the Patient) Date of Signature _____ _____ Legible Printed Name of Signer Telephone Number of Signer	
CLINICIAN signature **E** *Required* Fill in every line for valid Page 1.	Signature of physician, nurse practitioner or physician assistant confirms that this form accurately reflects his/her discussion(s) with the signer in Section D. X_____ _____ Signature of Physician, Nurse Practitioner, or Physician Assistant Date and Time of Signature _____ _____ Legible Printed Name of Signer Telephone Number of Signer	
Optional Expiration date (if any) and other information	This form does not expire unless expressly stated. *Expiration date (if any) of this form:* _____ Health Care Agent Printed Name _____ Telephone Number _____ Primary Care Provider Printed Name _____ Telephone Number _____	

SEND THIS FORM WITH THE PATIENT AT ALL TIMES.
HIPAA permits disclosure of MOLST to health care providers as necessary for treatment.

Patient's Name: _____ Patient's DOB _____ Medical Record # if applicable _____

F Mark one circle	**Statement of Patient Preferences for Other Medically-Indicated Treatments**		
	INTUBATION AND VENTILATION		
Mark one circle	○ Refer to Section B on Page 1	○ Use intubation and ventilation as marked in Section B, but short term only	○ Undecided ○ Did not discuss
	NON-INVASIVE VENTILATION (e.g. Continuous Positive Airway Pressure - CPAP)		
Mark one circle	○ Refer to Section B on Page 1	○ Use non-invasive ventilation as marked in Section B, but short term only	○ Undecided ○ Did not discuss
	DIALYSIS		
Mark one circle	○ No dialysis	○ Use dialysis ○ Use dialysis, but short term only	○ Undecided ○ Did not discuss
	ARTIFICIAL NUTRITION		
Mark one circle	○ No artificial nutrition	○ Use artificial nutrition ○ Use artificial nutrition, but short term only	○ Undecided ○ Did not discuss
	ARTIFICIAL HYDRATION		
Mark one circle	○ No artificial hydration	○ Use artificial hydration ○ Use artificial hydration, but short term only	○ Undecided ○ Did not discuss
	Other treatment preferences specific to the patient's medical condition and care _____ _____		

PATIENT or patient's representative signature G *Required* Mark one circle and fill in every line for valid Page 2.	**Mark one circle below to indicate who is signing Section G:** o Patient o Health Care Agent o Guardian* o Parent/Guardian* of minor Signature of patient confirms this form was signed of patient's own free will and reflects his/her wishes and goals of care as expressed to the Section H signer. Signature by the patient's representative (indicated above) confirms that this form reflects his/her assessment of the patient's wishes and goals of care, or if those wishes are unknown, his/her assessment of the patient's best interests. *A guardian can sign only to the extent permitted by MA law. Consult legal counsel with questions about a guardian's authority.*

	Signature of Patient (or Person Representing the Patient)	Date of Signature
	Legible Printed Name of Signer	Telephone Number of Signer

CLINICIAN signature H *Required* Fill in every line for valid Page 2.	Signature of physician, nurse practitioner or physician assistant confirms that this form accurately reflects his/her discussion(s) with the signer in Section G.	
	Signature of Physician, Nurse Practitioner, or Physician Assistant	Date and Time of Signature
	Legible Printed Name of Signer	Telephone Number of Signer

Additional Instructions For Health Care Professionals

→ Follow orders listed in A, B and C and honor preferences listed in F until there is an opportunity for a clinician to review as described below.
→ Any change to this form requires the form to be voided and a new form to be signed. To void the form, write VOID in large letters across both sides of the form. *If no new form is completed, no limitations on treatment are documented and full treatment may be provided.*
→ Re-discuss the patient's goals for care and treatment preferences as clinically appropriate to disease progression, at transfer to a new care setting or level of care, or if preferences change. Revise the form when needed to accurately reflect treatment preferences.
→ The patient or health care agent (if the patient lacks capacity), guardian*, or parent/guardian* of a minor can revoke the MOLST form at any time and/or request and receive previously refused medically-indicated treatment. *A guardian can sign only to the extent permitted by MA law. Consult legal counsel with questions about a guardian's authority.*

PAGE INTENTIONALLY LEFT BLANK

**MASSACHUSETTS DEPARTMENT OF PUBLIC HEALTH
OFFICE OF EMERGENCY MEDICAL SERVICES**

CCFORM_INSERT
2/2007

COMFORT CARE / DO NOT RESUSCITATE ("DNR") ORDER VERIFICATION

PATIENT'S LAST NAME	
PATIENT'S FIRST NAME	PATIENT'S MIDDLE NAME OR INITIAL
DATE OF BIRTH (MM/DD/YYYY) GENDER ☐ M ☐ F	
STREET OR RESIDENTIAL ADDRESS	
CITY	STATE	ZIP CODE (5 or 9 digits)
LAST NAME OF GUARDIAN OR HEALTH CARE AGENT (If applicable)	
FIRST NAME OF GUARDIAN OR HEALTH CARE AGENT	MIDDLE NAME OR INITIAL

PATIENT/GUARDIAN/HHEALTH CARE AGENT STATEMENT (SIGNATURE AND DATE REQUIRED)

I _____ (☐patient ☐ guardian ☐health care agent) verify that the above named patient has a **current and valid Do Not Resuscitate order** ("DNR order"). I understand that by signing this form, the DNR order, if current and valid, will be recognized in out-of-hospital settings and the COMFORT CARE / Do Not Resuscitate Order Verification Protocol will be followed by emergency medical services personnel.

_____   _____
Signature of Patient/Guardian/Health Care Agent   Date

PHYSICIAN / NURSE PRACTICIONER (NP) / PHYSICIAN ASSISTANT (PA) VERIFICATION (PHYSICIAN / NP / PA SIGNATURE AND DATES ALWAYS REQUIRED)

I am an attending physician / NP / PA for the above named patient. I verify that the above named patient has a current and valid Do Not Resuscitate order, issued on _____

This DNR order ☐ does ☐ does not have an expiration date. If there is an expiration date, it is indicated below, and this verification form also expires on that date.

I hereby direct that all emergency medical services personnel comply with the Massachusetts Department of Public Health, Office of Emergency Medical Services' COMFORT CARE / Do Not Resuscitate Order Verification Protocol with regard to the above named patient.

_____
Signature of Physician / NP / PA

Print Name of Physician / NP / PA | Effective Date of CC / DNR Order Verification | Expiration Date (if any) of DNR Order and CC/DNR Order Verification

Address of Physician / NP / PA

Telephone Number of Physician / NP / PA

OPTIONAL BRACELET INSERTS	
Attention Physician/NP/PA If used, enter information or print legibly. Physician/NP/ PA must sign, tear off strip, fold, trim, and insert in bracelet. **Massachusetts** **Comfort Care/DNR Order Verification**	Pat. Name _____ Gender M ☐ F ☐ Pat. DOB: _____ Expir. Date: _____ Tel. ___-___-___ MD/NP/PA _____ Signature _____
Attention Physician/NP/PA If used, enter information or print legibly. Physician/NP/ PA must sign, tear off strip, fold, trim, and insert in bracelet. **Massachusetts** **Comfort Care/DNR Order Verification**	Pat. Name _____ Gender M ☐ F ☐ Pat. DOB: _____ Expir. Date: _____ Tel. ___-___-___ MD/NP/PA _____ Signature _____
Attention Physician/NP/PA If used, enter information or print legibly. Physician/NP/ PA must sign, tear off strip, fold, trim, and insert in bracelet. **Massachusetts** **Comfort Care/DNR Order Verification**	Pat. Name _____ Gender M ☐ F ☐ Pat. DOB: _____ Expir. Date: _____ Tel. ___-___-___ MD/NP/PA _____ Signature _____
Attention Physician/NP/PA If used, enter information or print legibly. Physician/NP/ PA must sign, tear off strip, fold, trim, and insert in bracelet. **Massachusetts** **Comfort Care/DNR Order Verification**	Pat. Name _____ Gender M ☐ F ☐ Pat. DOB: _____ Expir. Date: _____ Tel. ___-___-___ MD/NP/PA _____ Signature _____

CHAPTER 13
FORM 7: DURABLE POWER OF ATTORNEY

FORM LETS PERSON GIVE POWER OVER THEIR PROPERTY AND MONEY

This form lets a person give power to someone to let them do things with the person's money, property, debt, and other things. Many people call this form the "Financial Power of Attorney" form.

FORM GIVES POWER TO LET SOMEONE CONTROL PROPERTY AND MONEY

The form lets a person (who is called in the form the "Principal") give power to someone (who is called in the form the "Agent" or "Attorney-in-Fact") to control the person's property, money, and other things. Doing this form can let the Agent for a person help use accounts, pay bills, buy or sell things, sign contracts, take out debt, hire workers, and get information from banks and others. Often named as Agent is a trusted person like a spouse, other relative, or a close friend. Doing this form might avoid need for a nursing home, guardian, conservator, or other serious thing. This form is called a "general" power of attorney since the power given is broad covering many areas, and the form is called "durable" since power of the form continues even if a person is later incapacitated. Note, a person until they are incapacitated usually can just overrule their Agent or fire the Agent if they notice a problem.

CAN GIVE INSTRUCTIONS OR LIMIT POWERS BUT FEW PEOPLE DO THIS

People can modify the form to add instructions or limit powers, but this is rare and full power is often given since the person named is trusted and banks and others may not obey the form if things aren't clear.

DUE TO RISKS MANY SKIP THIS FORM OR CONSULT A LAWYER

Many people skip this form or first see a lawyer. Using this form is risky and can lead to major harm since the Agent can be waste money, commit fraud or theft, or by carelessness allow some other harms. An Agent has a duty to be loyal and act reasonably and can be sued for any harm, but they may later be out of money to pay for misconduct. Usually banks and others can't be blamed for obeying an Agent's orders. The law is complex and basic acts of an Agent may be fine like paying bills, but some acts may be improper like making gifts, risky investments, or unusual acts. It is best a person not the Agent does anything unusual.

PERSON SIGNS FORM WITH A NOTARY

This form must be signed by a person when in front of a person who is a notary, and then the notary notarizes and also signs. The completed form can be kept by a person till needed but often it is quickly given to the Agent getting power to use if needed. To cancel the form a person usually tells the Agent it is canceled and takes back any copies and maybe tells all places that saw the form that it is now canceled.

DURABLE POWER OF ATTORNEY

I _____
(insert name and address) appoint _____
_____(insert name and address of the person appointed) as my agent (attorney-in-fact) to act for me in any way including in any way which I myself could do if I were personally present.

This instrument is to be construed and interpreted as a general durable power of attorney that is effective immediately.

THIS POWER OF ATTORNEY IS DURABLE AND SHALL NOT BE AFFECTED BY SUBSEQUENT DISABILITY OR INCAPACITY OF ME THE PRINCIPAL, OR BY LAPSE OF TIME.

(Optional) Instructions for agent: _____
_____
_____
_____

I agree any third party who receives a copy of this document may act under it. Revocation of power of attorney is not effective as to a third party until they learn of the revocation. I agree to indemnify the third party for any claims that arise against the third party because of reliance on this power of attorney.

SIGNATURE

Signed this _____ day of _____, 20____.

_____
Signature

NOTARY

Commonwealth of Massachusetts

_____, ss.

On this date, _____, before me, the undersigned notary public, personally appeared _____, proved to me through satisfactory evidence of identification, which was _____, to be the person whose name is signed on the preceding document, and swore under the pains and penalties of perjury that the foregoing statements are true.

Notary:_____

CHAPTER 14
FORM 8: TEMPORARY AGENT APPOINTMENT
(FOR MINOR CHILD)

FORM LETS PARENT GIVE POWER TO SOMEONE OVER MINOR CHILD

This form lets parents give power over a minor child under 18 to someone. Note, instead of a parent other people like a legal guardian or a legal custodian can use this form. Many states have a similar form but they usually call it a "Power Of Attorney Over A Minor" or similar name.

FORM CAN DESIGNATE SOMEONE TO HAVE POWER OVER CHILD

In the form a parent can name someone as "Temporary Agent" to have power over a child under age 18. This can let someone like a friend, relative, or teacher make decisions about a child's health care, school, food, discipline, home, and more. <u>This form is often used if parent is away from a child for work, school, sports, prison, drug treatment, immigration, military, long visit with family or friends, or if a child is in hospital and needs someone with authority nearby</u>. The form is usually <u>not</u> done for minor things like a babysitter, week long visit, daycare, or anytime a parent can come fast. A parent can usually fire or overrule the Agent at any time if they become aware of a decision they dislike. Note, letting someone else watch a child using this form is normal and not child abuse or child abandonment. Many states have a similar form they allow.

HAVING BOTH PARENTS DO THE FORM IS BEST BUT OFTEN SKIPPED

Massachusetts law prefers both parents sign to agree on a person to watch a child, with 1 parent signing at the top of the 2nd page and the 2nd parent signing at the end. But both parents signing is not officially needed if the 2nd parent is unable to watch a child or they can't be found. A parent can be unable to watch a child for many reasons like the parent has work, school, travel plans, bad health, or they have no room for a child to come and stay. No matter what even if just 1 parent signs the form usually doctors, teachers, and others don't object and they will usually follow the form without objection.

PERSON FORCED TO WATCH CHILD FOR MONTHS CAN DO DIFFERENT FORM

Massachusetts also has a "Caregiver Authorization Affidavit" form to let a person having to watch child in their home for over a month get legal power by them signing this form with no parent signature needed. This can be used for 2 years but a person forced to watch a child may want to do different legal things.

COMPLETE FORM BY SIGNING IN FRONT OF 2 WITNESSES

This form must be signed by at least 1 parent with 2 persons acting as witnesses. Witnesses must be at least age 18 and can't be named as Agent in the form. The person getting power later should sign the "Acknowledgement" spot before they act. The form when signed can be kept by a parent till needed but often it is quickly given to the Agent to use if needed. To cancel the form a parent should tell the person who got power and take back copies, and then maybe tell everyone that saw the form that it's cancelled. Note, instead of a parent other people like a legal guardian or a legal custodian can also use this form.

TEMPORARY AGENT APPOINTMENT
(FOR MINOR CHILD)

Massachusetts General Laws Chapter 190B, § 5-103

1. **APPOINTING PARTY** (Parent/custodian/guardian)

I, _____, residing at _____,
am the ☐ parent ☐ legal guardian ☐ legal custodian of the minor child(ren) listed below.
I do hereby appoint _____, residing at _____
_____ as temporary agent to exercise any power regarding the care, custody, or property [except the power to consent to marriage or adoption and any additional acts prohibited below], that I possess relative to the minor child(ren) whose names and dates of birth are:

name	date of birth	name	date of birth

The agent may NOT do the following: (*If there are any specific acts you do not want the agent to perform, please state those acts here.*) _____
_____

The following statements are true: (*Please read*)
- There are no court orders in effect that would prohibit me from exercising or conferring the rights and responsibilities that I wish to confer upon the agent. (*If you are the guardian or custodian, please attach the court order appointing you.*)
- I confer these rights and responsibilities freely and knowingly in order to provide for the child(ren) and not as a result of pressure, threats, or payments by any person or agency.
- I understand that, if the affidavit is amended or revoked, I must provide the amended affidavit or revocation to all parties to whom I have provided the affidavit.

This document shall take effect only if and at such time as I become **incapacitated or unavailable** to make decisions for my child. Proof of my incapacitation or unavailability may be made through the attestation of my healthcare professional or through attestation of my agent.

This document shall remain in effect 60 days after it takes effect or until I notify the agent in writing that I have amended or revoked it.

Check applicable statements:

☐ The non-appointing parent has given consent (*See page 4*)

☐ I have not attached the non-appointing parent consent because the non-appointing parent is:
(*The non-appointing, or other parent, does not have to give permission if one of the following statements is true*)
☐ deceased
☐ whereabouts unknown
☐ unwilling to provide care for the minor child
☐ unable to provide care for the minor child

I hereby affirm that the above statements are true and correct to the best of my knowledge.

Appointing Party Signature:_____ Date: _____
(parent/guardian/custodian)

Printed Name: _____ Telephone number: _____

2. WITNESSES TO APPOINTING PARTY SIGNATURE
(To be signed by persons over the age of 18 who are not the designated agent.)

_____   _____
Witness #1 Signature   Witness #2 Signature

_____   _____
Printed name   Printed name

_____   _____
Address and telephone number   Address and telephone number

3. TEMPORARY AGENT ACKNOWLEDGMENT *(To be signed and completed by agent)*

I, _____, hereby accept this Temporary Agent Appointment.

I am at least 18 years of age.

I understand that I may, without obtaining further consent from a parent, legal custodian, or legal guardian of the child(ren), exercise power relative to the child(ren), except those powers prohibited above.

I understand that, if the affidavit is amended or revoked, I must provide the amended affidavit or revocation to all parties to whom I have provided this affidavit prior to further exercising any rights or responsibilities under the affidavit.

I hereby affirm that the above statements are true and correct to the best of my knowledge.

Signature:_____ Date: _____

Printed Name: _____ Telephone number: _____

4. NONAPPOINTING PARENT CONSENT *(The other parent must give permission if you know where they are and they are willing and able to care for the child)*

I, _____, residing at _____, am the nonappointing parent of the child(ren). I consent to the designation of _____ to be a temporary agent for my child(ren). I understand that the temporary agent will have any power regarding the care, custody, or property of the child(ren), [except as stated in Section 1].

Signature:_____ Date: _____

Printed Name: _____ Telephone number: _____

CHAPTER 15
FORM 9: FINAL WISHES ABOUT BODILY REMAINS

LETS ORDERS BE GIVEN ON FUNERAL, BURIAL, CREMATION, AND MORE
This form lets A person give orders on what should be done with their bodily remains after death and related matters like funeral, burial, cremation, ceremonies, and more.

IN FORM CAN GIVE ORDERS FOR AFTER DEATH THAT MUST BE FOLLOWED
Massachusetts law lets a person give written orders about their funeral and related matters. This can include burial, cremation, ceremonies, religious services, tombstone, and buying goods and services for any of this. Any pre-paid or pre-arranged services however probably will be done unless a person while alive contacts the company they paid and cancels things. Payment for these things comes from pre-paid funeral accounts, insurance, and decedent's or estate's money and property, and Executor and family legally must help arrange payment so long as a person left enough money and property to pay for what they wanted. <u>Matters not covered in writing are left to closest family member to decide (in order this is spouse, parent, adult child, and brothers or sisters)</u>.

SIGN FORM WITH 1 WITNESS
The form must be signed by a person in front of a witness who is at least age 18 who then signs it too. A person usually should keep the form in a place it can be found <u>very quickly</u> within just 1 or 2 days of death. It may help to tell people where to find the form. A person can cancel the form by ripping it up or marking it cancelled, and then sometimes the person tells all persons who have been shown the form it is canceled.

FINAL WISHES ABOUT BODILY REMAINS

(Title 239 of the Code of Massachusetts Regulations, section 3.09)

This form should be signed before a witness and then given to someone or kept in a safe place so people will have access to it within days of death.

Pre-arranged services especially pre-paid funeral and other contracts a person has entered into and not cancelled will be followed even if they conflict with the instructions given below.

INSTRUCTIONS. I, _____, hereby state in this witnessed writing the following instructions concerning funeral, cremation, burial, and related matters: _____

_____

_____

_____

_____

_____

_____

_____

_____

_____

_____

_____

_____

_____

_____

_____

SIGNED: _____   **DATED:** _____

WITNESS

SIGNATURE OF WITNESS: _____

APPENDIX:
SAMPLE FILLED OUT LEGAL FORMS

TO GET FORMS TO USE PEOPLE CAN:
  (1) PHOTOCOPY BOOK PAGES,
  (2) TEAR OUT PAGES FROM A BOOK, OR
  (3) DOWNLOAD BOOK WITH FORMS FROM WWW.DAVENPORTPUBLISHING.COM,
  AND USUALLY USING PDF FORM IS BEST TO AVOID SPACING/FORMAT CHANGES.

EMAIL ANY COMMENTS TO DAVENPORTPRESS@GMAIL.COM.

On the next pages to show how it can be done are some sample filled out legal forms.

People can add words to legal forms by computer or typewriter to be neater, but many people just by hand use pen, marker, or pencil to handwrite words into forms.

It is not required but better if signatures and dates are in ink or marker (not pencil).

Many parts of the forms especially spaces for Will gifts can be left empty and unfilled.

Anyone can fill in the words in a legal form not just the person doing the form, like a friend with neat writing can fill in all the words, addresses, and dates that are needed. Only the signatures must be done by each person doing the form for themselves.

When adding words in a form any of these is a fine way to do this:
  "I appoint ___John Doe___ as Agent",
  "I appoint ___John Doe___ as Agent",
  "I appoint John Doe as Agent".

When doing forms it may help to know "respectively" means "in the order just stated".

People need not worry about neatness or small mistakes, and a document is usually fine if those people who knew person during their life can tell the likely meaning.

Sample Filled Out Form : Will (Standard)
with Gifts section skipped to not bother making small gifts
LAST WILL AND TESTAMENT

I, __Paul Samuel Maxwell__ , of __Bristol County__ , Massachusetts do revoke all prior Wills and testamentary documents and do make, publish, and declare this as my Will. I am of sound mind and under no duress or undue influence and acting voluntarily.

1. LIVING SPOUSE AND CHILDREN. To show I am mentally fit and have sufficient memory to do a Will I do say I now have the following living spouse and living children:

_____ none _____
_____.

2. GIFTS. I give these gifts in this Will, but to get a gift in this section the recipient must survive me except as otherwise stated below.

I give _____ to _____.
I give _____ to _____.
I give _____ to _____.
I give _____ to _____.
I give _____ to _____.
I give _____ to _____.

3. SEPARATE WRITINGS. I may do writings separate from this Will to gift tangible personal property as allowed by state law, and all such writings should be followed. But any such writing not found within 90 days of my death is canceled and has no effect. A gift in such a writing to a person who does not survive me is canceled and has no effect. This Will does not revoke any such writings that now exist.

4. RESIDUE. The rest, residue, and remainder of my estate, and anything else, I give:

a) to __Susan Lee Maxwell my sister__ who survive me and with persons just named who survive me taking the share of non-survivors, then if anything remains

b) to __Oscar Adam Maxwell and Mary Ann Tabor__ and if any of those just now named do not survive me their part goes to their lineal descendants per stirpes.

5. ADMINISTRATION. I nominate and appoint __Susan Lee Maxwell__ as Personal Representative including for me, my Will, and my estate.

6. MISCELLANEOUS. The following applies to this Will and generally.

In this Will no part left unfilled is a mistake including spaces in the residue clause.

The facts support and I want Massachusetts state law to apply to this Will and my estate. The term state and references to this include the Commonwealth of Massachusetts.

I order that my just debts, funeral and related expenses, and taxes be paid as soon after my death as practical but only those items my Personal Representative chooses to pay.

Priority of Will gifts of the same type is based on the order they are made in this Will.

The words give and gift also means a devise, bequest, grant, legacy, or similar.

I am intentionally not providing by Will or other ways for some family, including I am not providing for some children of mine and also children of a deceased child of mine.

If a Will gift reasonably mentions survival then survival is an absolute condition and anti-lapse laws or similar provisions have no effect and without survival the gift lapses. Unless a Will gift specifies otherwise if a Will gift goes to multiple recipients if any do not survive me the part to them lapses and instead goes to other surviving recipients.

No earlier transfer reduces a Will gift unless I usually called it a loan or advancement.

In this Will any gendered word includes all genders, and the singular includes the plural and vice versa, and they can mean a single person or many persons.

Unless a Will specifically says otherwise a secured debt including a mortgage or lien shall not be paid off including by a Personal Representative or in probate, and a recipient of a Will gift of property takes it subject to debts. Also, no recipient of property who may lose it or who pays to keep it may have my estate or others pay or do exoneration.

If I somehow lost ownership of an item in a specific Will gift the gift is extinguished.

I request and authorize any informal, summary, and quick probate or similar action. Any Personal Representative may act independently with no supervision of any court, including independent administration, and with no inventory, appraisal, or other action.

I give any Personal Representative the a) fullest authority, discretion, and powers allowed by state law, b) power to lease, sell, mortgage, convey, or keep property including real property in a manner and time they deem helpful or proper, and c) authority to settle or pay claims or debts in the time and manner they choose. Any Personal Representative or other fiduciary shall have all powers and authorities that may be given by statute or common law in any jurisdiction they may act, including under Massachusetts law.

Any Guardian of any type, Conservator, Custodian, or other person managing a minor's property or money may use or invade the principal and sell property without court action.

If context permits the terms Personal Representative and Executor and Administrator are interchangeable, Conservator and Guardian of the Estate and Guardian of Property and Custodian are interchangeable, and residue and residuary are interchangeable. Any such person may stand in the place of and have all powers like the others named here.

The residue includes lapsed or failed gifts, insurance paid to the estate, digital assets, inheritances owed me, and all I had power of appointment or testamentary disposition over.

Any Personal Representative may access, manage, delete, modify, transfer, and otherwise control any digital accounts and assets I had any interest in or power over.

Any Personal Representative, Executor, Administrator, Guardian of any type like for a person or estate, Conservator, Custodian, and any other fiduciary under this Will or otherwise shall qualify and serve without bond, surety, security, surety bond, or similar.

If evidence does not show it likely a person survived me by 120 hours (5 days) then for this Will and my estate they shall be deemed in all ways as having died before me.

If part of this Will is by law invalid or unenforceable other provisions remain in effect.

Any Personal Representative may at any time transfer money or property of a minor under age 18 to a Custodian to serve under the Massachusetts Uniform Transfers to Minors Act or similar law anywhere, and may pick a person to be Custodian including themselves.

TESTATOR

In witness whereof, I, _Paul Samual Maxwell_, the Testator, sign my name to this instrument this __8th__ day of __June__, 20__22__, and being first duly sworn, do hereby declare to the undersigned authority that I sign and execute this instrument as my Will and that I sign it willingly, that I execute it as my free and voluntary act for the purposes therein expressed, and that I am 18 years of age or older, of sound mind, and under no constraint or undue influence.

Paul Samuel Maxwell
Signature of Testator

WITNESSES

We, __Susan Ann Moon__ and __Eve Mable Smith__, Witnesses, sign our names to this instrument, being first duly sworn, and do hereby declare to the undersigned authority that the Testator signs and executes this instrument as the Testator's Will and that the Testator signs it willingly, and that each of us in the presence and hearing of the Testator hereby signs this Will to do the act of witnessing the Testator's signing, and that to the best of our knowledge the Testator is 18 years of age or older, of sound mind, and under no constraint or undue influence.

Susan Ann Moon   14 2nd Street, Springfield, MA 02843
Signature of Witness #1   Address of Witness #1

Eve Mable Smith   35 Buffalo Road, Denver, Colorado 80101
Signature of Witness #2   Address of Witness #2

Sample Filled Out Form : Will (Guardian)
with many gifts written in Gifts section, Guardian Clause used, and Residue Clause using percentages

LAST WILL AND TESTAMENT

I, __Paul Brian Baker__ of __Plymouth County__, Massachusetts, do revoke all prior Wills and testamentary documents and do make, publish, and declare this as my Will. I am of sound mind and under no duress or undue influence and acting voluntarily.

1. LIVING SPOUSE AND CHILDREN. To show I am mentally fit and have sufficient memory to do a Will I do say I now have the following living spouse and living children:

_____Ruth May Baker wife_____ _____Oscar Elliot Baker young son_____
_____ Karen Lisa Lundy daughter_____ Derek Rupert Baker son _____.

2. GIFTS. I give these gifts in this Will, but to get a gift in this section the recipient must survive me except as otherwise stated below.

I give _____big oak table_____ to _____Anne J. Smith_____.

I give __$5,000 and Ford Truck__ to __Loretta Marsha Baxter__.

I give __buildings, land, and fixtures at 63 Wentworth Road, Boston, Massachusetts,__ to __Kenneth Alan Ford__.

I give __all real property and fixtures I own in Middlesex County in Massachusetts__ to __Amy Marie Fox and Pamela Sue Fox__.

I give __903 Iceberg Road, Anchorage, Alaska__ to __James Eric Hanson__.

I give __Irish jewelry and my wedding ring__ to __Mary Natalie Swanson__.

I give __all jewelry not given above__ to __Kay Baxter and Mary Baxter__.

I give __$781.35__ to __Mary Natalie Swanson and Kevin Kilby__.

I give __Wells Fargo acct ending in #8923__ to __Lawrence Deer a hunting buddy__.

I give __all spare tires and auto parts__ to __Victor Perez my mechanic__.

3. SEPARATE WRITINGS. I may do writings separate from this Will to gift tangible personal property as allowed by state law, and all such writings should be followed. But any such writing not found within 90 days of my death is canceled and has no effect. A gift in such a writing to a person who does not survive me is canceled and has no effect. This Will does not revoke any such writings that now exist.

4. RESIDUE. The rest, residue, and remainder of my estate, and anything else, I give:
  a) to _____Ruth May Baker_____ who survive me and with persons just named who survive me taking the share of non-survivors, then if anything remains
  b) to _50% to Oscar Elliot Baker, 35% to Karen Lisa Lundy, 5% to Mary Sue Baker, and ____10% to Luis Sanchez my friend_____ and if any of those just now named do not survive me their part goes to their lineal descendants per stirpes.

5. ADMINISTRATION. I nominate and appoint __Ruth May Baker_____ as Personal Representative including for me, my Will, and my estate.

6. GUARDIAN. I name, nominate, and appoint _Amanda Sue Brubaker my sister_____ to be Guardian of any minor child of mine and to have care, authority, custody, and other control of them (including as Guardian of the Person). I name this same person to be Conservator for any minor child and to have care, control, and power over their property, money, and estate (including as Guardian of the Estate).

7. MISCELLANEOUS. The following applies to this Will and generally.
  In this Will no part left unfilled is a mistake including spaces in the residue clause.
  The facts support and I want Massachusetts state law to apply to this Will and my estate. The term state and references to this include the Commonwealth of Massachusetts.
  I order that my just debts, funeral and related expenses, and taxes be paid as soon after my death as practical but only those items my Personal Representative chooses to pay.
  Priority of Will gifts of the same type is based on the order they are made in this Will.
  The words give and gift also means a devise, bequest, grant, legacy, or similar.
  I am intentionally not providing by Will or other ways for some family, including I am not providing for some children of mine and also children of a deceased child of mine.
  If a Will gift reasonably mentions survival then survival is an absolute condition and anti-lapse laws or similar provisions have no effect and without survival the gift lapses. Unless a Will gift specifies otherwise if a Will gift goes to multiple recipients if any do not survive me the part to them lapses and instead goes to other surviving recipients.
  No earlier transfer reduces a Will gift unless I usually called it a loan or advancement.
  In this Will any gendered word includes all genders, and the singular includes the plural and vice versa, and they can mean a single person or many persons.
  Unless a Will specifically says otherwise a secured debt including a mortgage or lien shall not be paid off including by a Personal Representative or in probate, and a recipient of a Will gift of property takes it subject to debts. Also, no recipient of property who may lose it or who pays to keep it may have my estate or others pay or do exoneration.
  If I somehow lost ownership of an item in a specific Will gift the gift is extinguished.
  I request and authorize any informal, summary, and quick probate or similar action. Any Personal Representative may act independently with no supervision of any court, including independent administration, and with no inventory, appraisal, or other action.

Any Guardian of any type, Conservator, Custodian, or other person managing a minor's property or money may use or invade the principal and sell property without court action.

The residue includes lapsed or failed gifts, insurance paid to the estate, digital assets, inheritances owed me, and all I had power of appointment or testamentary disposition over.

Any Personal Representative may access, manage, delete, modify, transfer, and otherwise control any digital accounts and assets I had any interest in or power over.

Any Personal Representative, Executor, Administrator, Guardian of any type like for a person or estate, Conservator, Custodian, and any other fiduciary under this Will or otherwise shall qualify and serve without bond, surety, security, surety bond, or similar.

If evidence does not show it likely a person survived me by 120 hours (5 days) then for this Will and my estate they shall be deemed in all ways as having died before me.

If part of this Will is by law invalid or unenforceable other provisions remain in effect.

Any Personal Representative may at any time transfer money or property of a minor under age 18 to a Custodian to serve under the Massachusetts Uniform Transfers to Minors Act or similar law anywhere, and may pick a person to be Custodian including themselves.

TESTATOR

In witness whereof, I, __Paul Brian Baker__, the Testator, sign my name to this instrument this __30th__ day of __December__, 20__21__, and being first duly sworn, do hereby declare to the undersigned authority that I sign and execute this instrument as my Will and that I sign it willingly, that I execute it as my free and voluntary act for the purposes therein expressed, and that I am 18 years of age or older, of sound mind, and under no constraint or undue influence.

Paul Brian Baker
Signature of Testator

WITNESSES

We, __Olivia Anna Paulson__ and __Matthew John Paulson__, Witnesses, sign our names to this instrument, being first duly sworn, and do hereby declare to the undersigned authority that the Testator signs and executes this instrument as the Testator's Will and that the Testator signs it willingly, and that each of us in the presence and hearing of the Testator hereby signs this Will to do the act of witnessing the Testator's signing, and that to the best of our knowledge the Testator is 18 years of age or older, of sound mind, and under no constraint or undue influence.

Olivia Anna Paulson   __82 Forest Road, Boston, MA 01004__
Signature of Witness #1   Address of Witness #1

Matthew John Paulson   __82 Forest Road, Boston, MA 01004__
Signature of Witness #2   Address of Witness #2

Sample Filled Out Form : Will (Guardian)
with Gifts section left unused and, then, the Residue Clause done only using 2nd space so as to gift to all branches of person's descendants equally

LAST WILL AND TESTAMENT

I, __Thomas Roger Tedford__ of __Worcester County__, Massachusetts do revoke all prior Wills and testamentary documents and do make, publish, and declare this as my Will. I am of sound mind and under no duress or undue influence and acting voluntarily.

1. LIVING SPOUSE AND CHILDREN. To show I am mentally fit and have sufficient memory to do a Will I do say I now have the following living spouse and living children: __Mary Paula Tedford my daughter__ __Gina Lola Smith my daughter__ _____.

2. GIFTS. I give these gifts in this Will, but to get a gift in this section the recipient must survive me except as otherwise stated below.

I give _____ to _____.
I give _____ to _____.
I give _____ to _____.
I give _____ to _____.
I give _____ to _____.
I give _____ to _____.

SKIPPED

3. SEPARATE WRITINGS. I may do writings separate from this Will to gift tangible personal property as allowed by state law, and all such writings should be followed. But any such writing not found within 90 days of my death is canceled and has no effect. A gift in such a writing to a person who does not survive me is canceled and has no effect. This Will does not revoke any such writings that now exist.

4. RESIDUE. The rest, residue, and remainder of my estate, and anything else, I give:
  a) to _____ who survive me and with persons just named who survive me taking the share of non-survivors, then if anything remains
  b) to __Brian Alan Tedford my deceased son,__ __Mary Paula Tedford my daughter,__ __and Gina Lola Smith my daughter__ and if any of those just now named do not survive me their part goes to their lineal descendants per stirpes.

5. ADMINISTRATION. I nominate and appoint ___Mary Paula Tedford___
as Personal Representative including for me, my Will, and my estate.

6. MISCELLANEOUS. The following applies to this Will and generally.
    In this Will no part left unfilled is a mistake including spaces in the residue clause.
    The facts support and I want Massachusetts state law to apply to this Will and my estate. The term state and references to this include the Commonwealth of Massachusetts.
    I order that my just debts, funeral and related expenses, and taxes be paid as soon after my death as practical but only those items my Personal Representative chooses to pay.
    Priority of Will gifts of the same type is based on the order they are made in this Will.
    The words give and gift also means a devise, bequest, grant, legacy, or similar.
    I am intentionally not providing by Will or other ways for some family, including I am not providing for some children of mine and also children of a deceased child of mine.
    If a Will gift reasonably mentions survival then survival is an absolute condition and anti-lapse laws or similar provisions have no effect and without survival the gift lapses. Unless a Will gift specifies otherwise if a Will gift goes to multiple recipients if any do not survive me the part to them lapses and instead goes to other surviving recipients.
    No earlier transfer reduces a Will gift unless I usually called it a loan or advancement.
    In this Will any gendered word includes all genders, and the singular includes the plural and vice versa, and they can mean a single person or many persons.
    Unless a Will specifically says otherwise a secured debt including a mortgage or lien shall not be paid off including by a Personal Representative or in probate, and a recipient of a Will gift of property takes it subject to debts. Also, no recipient of property who may lose it or who pays to keep it may have my estate or others pay or do exoneration.
    If I somehow lost ownership of an item in a specific Will gift the gift is extinguished.
    I request and authorize any informal, summary, and quick probate or similar action. Any Personal Representative may act independently with no supervision of any court, including independent administration, and with no inventory, appraisal, or other action.
    I give any Personal Representative the a) fullest authority, discretion, and powers allowed by state law, b) power to lease, sell, mortgage, convey, or keep property including real property in a manner and time they deem helpful or proper, and c) authority to settle or pay claims or debts in the time and manner they choose. Any Personal Representative or other fiduciary shall have all powers and authorities that may be given by statute or common law in any jurisdiction they may act, including under Massachusetts law.
    Any Guardian of any type, Conservator, Custodian, or other person managing a minor's property or money may use or invade the principal and sell property without court action.
    If context permits the terms Personal Representative and Executor and Administrator are interchangeable, Conservator and Guardian of the Estate and Guardian of Property and Custodian are interchangeable, and residue and residuary are interchangeable. Any such person may stand in the place of and have all powers like the others named here.
    The residue includes lapsed or failed gifts, insurance paid to the estate, digital assets,

inheritances owed me, and all I had power of appointment or testamentary disposition over.

Any Personal Representative may access, manage, delete, modify, transfer, and otherwise control any digital accounts and assets I had any interest in or power over.

Any Personal Representative, Executor, Administrator, Guardian of any type like for a person or estate, Conservator, Custodian, and any other fiduciary under this Will or otherwise shall qualify and serve without bond, surety, security, surety bond, or similar.

If evidence does not show it likely a person survived me by 120 hours (5 days) then for this Will and my estate they shall be deemed in all ways as having died before me.

If part of this Will is by law invalid or unenforceable other provisions remain in effect.

Any Personal Representative may at any time transfer money or property of a minor under age 18 to a Custodian to serve under the Massachusetts Uniform Transfers to Minors Act or similar law anywhere, and may pick a person to be Custodian including themselves.

TESTATOR

In witness whereof, I, _Thomas Roger Tedford_ , the Testator, sign my name to this instrument this _15th_ day of _March_ , 20_21_ , and being first duly sworn, do hereby declare to the undersigned authority that I sign and execute this instrument as my Will and that I sign it willingly, that I execute it as my free and voluntary act for the purposes therein expressed, and that I am 18 years of age or older, of sound mind, and under no constraint or undue influence.

Thomas Roger Tedford
Signature of Testator

WITNESSES

We, _Maria Bonita Buena_ and _Richard Max West_ , Witnesses, sign our names to this instrument, being first duly sworn, and do hereby declare to the undersigned authority that the Testator signs and executes this instrument as the Testator's Will and that the Testator signs it willingly, and that each of us in the presence and hearing of the Testator hereby signs this Will to do the act of witnessing the Testator's signing, and that to the best of our knowledge the Testator is 18 years of age or older, of sound mind, and under no constraint or undue influence.

Maria Bonita Buena   _101 Fox Rd., Apt. #35 Clayton, MA 01003_
Signature of Witness #1   Address of Witness #1

Richard Max West   _28 Miller Avenue, Pineville, MA 02361_
Signature of Witness #2   Address of Witness #2

Sample Filled Out Form : Will (Standard)
with Will modified to have a 1 Part Residue Clause

LAST WILL AND TESTAMENT

I, __John David Smith__, of __Essex County__, Massachusetts, do revoke all prior Wills and testamentary documents and do make, publish, and declare this as my Will. I am of sound mind and under no duress or undue influence and acting voluntarily.

1. LIVING SPOUSE AND CHILDREN. To show I am mentally fit and have sufficient memory to do a Will I do say I now have the following living spouse and living children:

___my son Adam Michael Smith___

2. GIFTS. I give these gifts in this Will, but to get a gift in this section the recipient must survive me except as otherwise stated below.

I give __$200__ to __each of my nieces and nephews so about $2,800 in total__.

I give __$400__ to __Garner Food Shelf in Boston, MA by the Zakim bridge__.

I give __$340__ to __my old church Trinity Catholic Church in Pueblo, Colorado__.

I give _____ to _____.

I give _____ to _____.

I give _____ to _____.

I give _____ to _____.

I give _____ to _____.

I give _____ to _____.

I give _____ to _____.

3. SEPARATE WRITINGS. I may do writings separate from this Will to gift tangible personal property as allowed by state law, and all such writings should be followed. But any such writing not found within 90 days of my death is canceled and has no effect. A gift in such a writing to a person who does not survive me is canceled and has no effect. This Will does not revoke any such writings that now exist.

4. RESIDUE. The rest, residue, and remainder of my estate, and anything else, I give to: ___Adam Michael Smith___ and ___Judy Paula Ford___ who survive me and if any of those just named do not survive me their part goes to their lineal descendants per stirpes.

5. ADMINISTRATION. I nominate and appoint ___Judy Paula Ford my sister___ as Personal Representative including for me, my Will, and my estate.

6. MISCELLANEOUS. The following applies to this Will and generally.

In this Will no part left unfilled is a mistake including spaces in the residue clause.

The facts support and I want Massachusetts state law to apply to this Will and my estate. The term state and references to this include the Commonwealth of Massachusetts.

I order that my just debts, funeral and related expenses, and taxes be paid as soon after my death as practical but only those items my Personal Representative chooses to pay.

Priority of Will gifts of the same type is based on the order they are made in this Will.

The words give and gift also means a devise, bequest, grant, legacy, or similar.

I am intentionally not providing by Will or other ways for some family, including I am not providing for some children of mine and also children of a deceased child of mine.

If a Will gift reasonably mentions survival then survival is an absolute condition and anti-lapse laws or similar provisions have no effect and without survival the gift lapses. Unless a Will gift specifies otherwise if a Will gift goes to multiple recipients if any do not survive me the part to them lapses and instead goes to other surviving recipients.

No earlier transfer reduces a Will gift unless I usually called it a loan or advancement.

In this Will any gendered word includes all genders, and the singular includes the plural and vice versa, and they can mean a single person or many persons.

Unless a Will specifically says otherwise a secured debt including a mortgage or lien shall not be paid off including by a Personal Representative or in probate, and a recipient of a Will gift of property takes it subject to debts. Also, no recipient of property who may lose it or who pays to keep it may have my estate or others pay or do exoneration.

If I somehow lost ownership of an item in a specific Will gift the gift is extinguished.

I request and authorize any informal, summary, and quick probate or similar action. Any Personal Representative may act independently with no supervision of any court, including independent administration, and with no inventory, appraisal, or other action.

Any Guardian of any type, Conservator, Custodian, or other person managing a minor's property or money may use or invade the principal and sell property without court action.

If context permits the terms Personal Representative and Executor and Administrator are interchangeable, Conservator and Guardian of the Estate and Guardian of Property and Custodian are interchangeable, and residue and residuary are interchangeable. Any such person may stand in the place of and have all powers like the others named here.

The residue includes lapsed or failed gifts, insurance paid to the estate, digital assets, inheritances owed me, and all I had power of appointment or testamentary disposition over.

Any Personal Representative may access, manage, delete, modify, transfer, and

otherwise control any digital accounts and assets I had any interest in or power over.

Any Personal Representative, Executor, Administrator, Guardian of any type like for a person or estate, Conservator, Custodian, and any other fiduciary under this Will or otherwise shall qualify and serve without bond, surety, security, surety bond, or similar.

If evidence does not show it likely a person survived me by 120 hours (5 days) then for this Will and my estate they shall be deemed in all ways as having died before me.

If part of this Will is by law invalid or unenforceable other provisions remain in effect.

Any Personal Representative may at any time transfer money or property of a minor under age 18 to a Custodian to serve under the Massachusetts Uniform Transfers to Minors Act or similar law anywhere, and may pick a person to be Custodian including themselves.

TESTATOR

In witness whereof, I, __John David Smith__, the Testator, sign my name to this instrument this _21st_ day of _____June_____, 20_23_ and being first duly sworn, do hereby declare to the undersigned authority that I sign and execute this instrument as my Will and that I sign it willingly, that I execute it as my free and voluntary act for the purposes therein expressed, and that I am 18 years of age or older, of sound mind, and under no constraint or undue influence.

_____*John David Smith*_____
Signature of Testator

WITNESSES

We, __Mark Elliot Potter__ and __Ann Paula Blom__, Witnesses, sign our names to this instrument, being first duly sworn, and do hereby declare to the undersigned authority that the Testator signs and executes this instrument as the Testator's Will and that the Testator signs it willingly, and that each of us in the presence and hearing of the Testator hereby signs this Will to do the act of witnessing the Testator's signing, and that to the best of our knowledge the Testator is 18 years of age or older, of sound mind, and under no constraint or undue influence.

__*Mark Elliot Potter*__   __24 Spruce St, Sherwood, MA 01026__
Signature of Witness #1   Address of Witness #1

__*Ann Paula Blom*__   __80 Oak Road, Edison, Massachusetts__
Signature of Witness #2   Address of Witness #2

Sample Filled Out Form : Self-Proving Affidavit

SELF-PROVING AFFIDAVIT

(Mass. Gen. Laws chapter 190B section 2-504)

THE STATE OF MASSACHUSETTS

COUNTY OF _____ESSEX_____

We, _____John David Smith_____, _____Mark Elliot Potter_____, and _____Ann Paula Blom_____ the Testator and the Witnesses, respectively, whose names are signed to the attached or foregoing instrument, being first duly sworn, do hereby declare to the undersigned authority that the Testator signed and executed the instrument as the Testator's Will and that the Testator had signed willingly, and that the Testator executed it as the Testator's free and voluntary act for the purposes therein expressed, and that each of the Witnesses, in the presence and hearing of the Testator, signed the Will to act as a witness and that to the best of the knowledge of each Witness the Testator was at that time 18 years of age or older, of sound mind, and under no constraint or undue influence.

John David Smith
Testator

Mark Elliot Potter
Witness

Ann Paula Blom
Witness

Subscribed, sworn to and acknowledged before me by , the testator, and subscribed and sworn to before me by _____John David Smith_____, the Testator, and _____Mark Elliot Potter_____ and _____Anna Paula Blom_____, the Witnesses, this __21st__ day of _____June_____, 20__23__.

(Seal)

MARIANNE PROVOST
Notary Public
COMMONWEALTH OF MASSACHUSETTS
My Commission Expires
December 3, 2027

Signed: *Marianne Provost*

Official capacity of officer:_____

Sample Filled Out Form : Tangible Personal Property Memorandum

TANGIBLE PERSONAL PROPERTY MEMORANDUM

In this writing are gifts of tangible personal property to occur at my death, but this writing if not found by someone within 90 days of my death is canceled.

I may do many pages of these writings which should all be seen as one document. If there are conflicts among such writings the provisions of the more recent writing will revoke the inconsistent provisions of a prior writing.

If a person getting a gift below does not survive me such gift is void and canceled.

DESCRIPTION OF PROPERTY	NAME OF PERSONS TO GET PROPERTY
1998 Ford Truck	to Kevin Swenson
1.3 carat diamond ring + Irish rings	to Ann Sue Reed
14 ft power boat + kayak + paddles	to L. Wheeler
Amish style bench	to Reba Stewart
glass table, telescope, umbrellas	to Wendy Stewart
Irish wood cups, oak platter, red vase	to Mary and Cindy Lott
painting of sailboat in storm	to Mary Lott
chainsaw with number 382937	to Mary Lott
chainsaw with number 89930	to Matt Smith
antique lanterns + repair kits	to Sue Wu maid at Hart Hotel
lamp kept on porch	to Mary Kay Poppler
sewing machines	to Mary Kay Poppler
rocking chair bought in Oregon	to Don Winkler boat mechanic
all fishing poles and fishing nets	to Joe "Fish" Hoss, fishing pal
hats at cabin	to Ken Baker
all clothing except hats at cabin	to Melissa and Arthur Smith
	to
	to

DATE: 8-15-2024   SIGNED: John David Smith